INTELLIGENCE ESSENTIALS FOR EVERYONE

By Lisa Krizan

JOINT MILITARY INTELLIGENCE COLLEGE

Books for Business
New York-Hong Kong

Intelligence Essentials for Everyone

by
Lisa Krizan

for the
Joint Military Intelligence College

ISBN: 0-89499-213-9

Reprinted from the 1999 edition

Books for Business
New York - Hong Kong
http://www.BusinessBooksInternational.com

CONTENTS

INTELLIGENCE ESSENTIALS FOR EVERYONE

Preface

The "importance of understanding" has become almost an obsession with significant portions of American business. There remain, however, many companies that attempt to operate as they traditionally have in the past — placing great faith in the owner's or manager's judgment as to what is required to remain competitive.

In this paper, the author has articulated clearly the fundamentals of sound intelligence practice and has identified some guidelines that can lead toward creation of a solid intelligence infrastructure. These signposts apply both to government intelligence and to business. Good intelligence should always be based on validated requirements, but it may be derived from a wide variety of sources, not all of which are reliable.

Understanding the needs of the consumer and the sources available enable an analyst to choose the correct methodology to arrive at useful answers. The author has laid out in clear, concise language a logical approach to creating an infrastructure for government and business. Every system will have flaws but this discussion should help the reader minimize those weaknesses. It is an important contribution to the education of government and business intelligence professionals.

James A. Williams, LTG, U.S. Army (Ret.)
Former Director, Defense Intelligence Agency

INTELLIGENCE ESSENTIALS FOR EVERYONE

Foreword

Decades of government intelligence experience and reflection on that experience are captured in this primer. Ms. Krizan combines her own findings on best practices in the intelligence profession with the discoveries and ruminations of other practitioners, including several Joint Military Intelligence College instructors and students who preceded her. Many of the selections she refers to are from documents that are out of print or have wrongly been assigned to a dustbin.

This primer reviews and reassesses Intelligence Community best practices with special emphasis on how they may be adopted by the private sector. The government convention of referring to intelligence users as "customers" suggests by itself the demonstrable similarities between government intelligence and business information support functions.

The genesis for this study was the author's discovery of a need to codify for the Intelligence Community certain basic principles missing from the formal training of intelligence analysts. At the same time, she learned of requests from the private sector for the same type of codified, government best practices for adaptation to the business world. As no formal mechanism existed for an exchange of these insights between the public and private sectors, Ms. Krizan developed this paper as an adjunct to her Master's thesis, *Benchmarking the Intelligence Process for the Private Sector.* Her thesis explores the rationale and mechanisms for benchmarking the intelligence process in government, and for sharing the resultant findings with the private sector.

Dr. Russell G. Swenson, Editor and Director, Office of Applied Research

PROLOGUE:
INTELLIGENCE SHARING
IN A NEW LIGHT

Education is the cheapest defense of a nation.
— Edmund Burke, 18th-century British philosopher

National Intelligence Meets Business Intelligence

This intelligence primer reflects the author's examination of dozens of unclassified government documents on the practice of intelligence over a period of nearly seven years. For the national security Intelligence Community (IC), it represents a concise distillation and clarification of the national intelligence function. To the private sector, it offers an unprecedented translation into lay terms of national intelligence principles and their application within and potentially outside of government.[1] Whereas "intelligence sharing" has traditionally been a government-to-government transaction, the environment is now receptive to government-private sector interaction.

The widespread trend toward incorporating government intelligence methodology into commerce and education was a primary impetus for publishing this document. As economic competition accelerates around the world, private businesses are initiating their own "business intelligence" (BI) or "competitive intelligence" services to advise their decisionmakers. Educators in business and academia are following suit, inserting BI concepts into professional training and college curricula.[2]

Whereas businesses in the past have concentrated on knowing the market and making the best product, they are shifting their focus to include knowing, and staying ahead of, competitors. This emphasis on competitiveness requires the sophisticated production and use of carefully analyzed information tailored to specific users; in other words, intelligence. But the use of intelligence as a strategic planning tool, common in government, is a skill that few companies have perfected.[3]

Although BI practitioners refer to the national security model of intelligence, they do not seek to conduct secret intelligence operations, which are limited by law to government

---

[1] For the purpose of this study, the author includes in national security intelligence those analogous activities conducted by law enforcement personnel at the federal, state, and local levels. Readers seeking further information on law enforcement applications of intelligence may wish to read Marilyn Peterson, *Applications in Criminal Analysis* (Westport, Connecticut: Greenwood Press, 1994). An additional resource is the International Association of Law Enforcement Intelligence Analysts. Local IALEIA chapters are listed on the Association's web site: http://www.ialeia.org.

[2] An authoritative guide to business intelligence practices is found in Larry Kahaner, *Competitive Intelligence: From Black Ops to Boardrooms — How Businesses Gather, Analyze and Use Information to Succeed in the Global Marketplace* (New York, NY: Simon and Schuster, 1996).

[3] Richard D'Aveni, "Hypercompetition," briefing to SCIP Conference, Alexandria, VA, 28 March 1996.

authorities. The Society of Competitive Intelligence Professionals (SCIP), headquartered in the Washington, DC area, is an international organization founded in 1986 to "assist members in enhancing their firms' competitiveness through a greater... understanding of competitor behaviors and future strategies as well as the market dynamics in which they do business."[4] SCIP's code of conduct specifically promotes ethical and legal BI practices.[5] The main focus of "collection" is on exploiting on-line and open-source information services, and the theme of "analysis" is to go beyond mere numerical and factual information, to interpretation of events for strategic decisionmaking.[6]

Large corporations are creating their own intelligence units, and a few are successful at performing analysis in support of strategic decisionmaking. Others are hiring BI contractors, or "out-sourcing" this function. However, the majority of businesses having some familiarity with BI are not able to conduct rigorous research and analysis for value-added reporting. According to University of Pittsburgh professor of Business Administration John Prescott, no theoretical framework exists for BI. He believes that most studies done lack the rigor that would come with following sound research-design principles. By his estimate, only one percent of companies have a research-design capability exploitable for BI applications.[7] At the same time, companies are increasingly opting to establish their own intelligence units rather than purchasing services from BI specialists. The implication of this trend is that BI professionals should be skilled in both intelligence and in a business discipline of value to the company.[8]

On the other hand, as businesses come to appreciate the value of intelligence about their competitors, they are increasingly realizing their own vulnerability to similar scrutiny. The private sector can therefore benefit from IC expertise in disciplines complementary to active intelligence production, namely defensive measures. The whole concept of openness regarding intelligence practices may hinge upon the counter-balancing effect of self-defense, particularly as practiced through information systems security (INFOSEC) and operations security (OPSEC).[9] Because the IC seeks to be a world leader in INFOSEC and OPSEC as well as intelligence production, defensive measures are an appropriate topic for dialogue between the public and private sectors.

The U.S. government INFOSEC Manual sums up the relationship between offense and defense in a comprehensive intelligence strategy in this way:

> In today's information age environment, control of information and information technology is vital. As the nation daily becomes more dependent on

---

[4] SCIP, *Competitive Intelligence Review*, 8, No. 3 (Fall 1997), unnumbered 8th page.

[5] SCIP, *1995 SCIP Membership Directory* (Alexandria, VA: SCIP, 1995), xxvii.

[6] Leila Kight, "Elements of CI Success," briefing to SCIP Conference, Alexandria, VA, 28 March, 1996.

[7] John Prescott, Professor of Business Administration, University of Pittsburgh, "Research," briefing to SCIP conference, Alexandria, VA, 28 March 1996.

[8] Jan Herring, "Strides in Institutionalizing BI in Businesses," briefing to SCIP Conference, Alexandria, VA, 28 March 1996.

[9] These concepts are addressed in Part IX.

networked information systems to conduct essential business, including military operations, government functions, and national and international economic enterprises, information infrastructures are assuming increased strategic importance. This has, in turn, given rise to the concept of information warfare (INFOWAR) — a new form of warfare directed toward attacking (offensive) or defending (defensive) such infrastructures.[10]

Giving citizens the tools they need to survive INFOWAR is one of the IC's explicit missions. This intelligence primer can assist that mission by offering a conceptual and practical "common operating environment" for business and government alike.[11]

Assessing and Exchanging Best Practices

In documenting the essentials of intelligence, this primer is an example of *benchmarking*, a widely used process for achieving quality in organizations, the use of which is a criterion for the business world's Malcolm Baldrige National Quality Award.[12] Benchmarking normally assesses best professional practices, developed and refined through experience, for carrying out an organization's core tasks.[13] An additional aim of benchmarking is to establish reciprocal relationships among best-in-class parties for the exchange of mutually beneficial information.[14] Because the IC is the *de facto* functional leader in the intelligence profession, and is publicly funded, it is obligated to lead both the government and private sector toward a greater understanding of the intelligence discipline.

In the mid-1990s, as national intelligence agencies began to participate in international benchmarking forums, individuals from the private sector began to request practical information on the intelligence process from IC representatives. The requestors were often participants in the growing BI movement and apparently sought to adapt IC methods to their own purposes. Their circumspect counterparts in the government were not prepared to respond to these requests, preferring instead to limit benchmarking relationships to common business topics, such as resource management.[15] Concurrently, the annual SCIP international conference highlighted the needs and capabilities of intelligence departments in the private sector.

---

[10] National Security Agency, *1995 INFOSEC Manual* (Ft. Meade, MD: NSA, 1995), para. C.1.

[11] Readers in doubt of the need for INFOSEC in the private sector may wish to study the real-world examples of INFOWAR battles and their implications for economic and personal security that author Winn Schwartau reveals in *Information Warfare: Chaos on the Electronic Superhighway*, (New York: Thunder's Mouth Press, 1994).

[12] A useful reference to benchmarking within the U.S. government is Jerry Frankenfield and Melissie Rumizen, *A Guide to Benchmarking* (Fort Meade, MD: National Security Agency (NSA), 12 July 1995). An overview of benchmarking in the private sector can be found in Dean Elmuti, Hanus Kathawaia, and Scott J. Lloyed, "The Benchmarking Process: Assessing Its Value and Limitations," *Industrial Management*, 39, No. 4 (July/August 1997): 12-19.

[13] Elmuti, Kathawaia and Lloyed, 12.

[14] Elmuti, Kathawaia and Lloyed, 13.

[15] Melissie C. Rumizen, Ph.D., Benchmarking Manager, National Security Agency, interview with the author, 2 April 1996.

Demand in the private sector for intelligence skills can be met through the application of validated intelligence practices presented in this document. Conversely, the business-oriented perspective on intelligence can be highly useful to government intelligence professionals. As a BI practitioner explains, every activity in the intelligence process must be related to a requirement, otherwise it is irrelevant.[16] Government personnel would benefit from this practical reminder in every training course and every work center. In the private sector, straying from this principle means wasting money and losing a competitive edge. The consequences of inefficient national intelligence can be costly on an even larger scale.

The basis for an IC benchmarking exchange with the private sector continues to grow. The Society of Competitive Intelligence Professionals is a clearinghouse for the review of private business intelligence practices, and therefore a champion of information sharing. Leading colleges and universities are beginning to offer coursework in intelligence methods, and in many cases intend to expand their offerings. Curriculum exchanges between private sector educators and the IC are encouraged by legislation and by Congressional Commission recommendations,[17] yet little such formal exchange has taken place.

Whereas government practitioners are the acknowledged subject-matter experts in intelligence methodology, the private sector offers a wealth of expertise in particular areas such as business management, technology, the global marketplace, and skills training. Each has valuable knowledge to share with the other, and experience gaps to fill. On the basis of these unique needs and capabilities, the public and private sectors can forge a new partnership in understanding their common responsibilities, and this primer may make a modest contribution toward the exchange of ideas.

The following chapters outline validated steps to operating an intelligence service for both the government and the private sector. In either setting, this document should prove useful as a basic curriculum for students, an on-the-job working aid for practitioners, and a reference tool for experienced professionals, especially those teaching or mentoring others. Although the primer does not exhaustively describe procedures for quality intelligence production or defensive measures, it does offer the business community fundamental concepts that can transfer readily from national intelligence to commercial applications, including competitive analysis, strategic planning and the protection of proprietary information. Universities may incorporate these ideas into their business, political science, and intelligence studies curricula to encourage and prepare students to become intelligence practitioners in commerce or government. For anyone outside of the

---

[16] David Harkleroad, "Actionable CI," briefing to SCIP Conference, Alexandria, VA, 28 March 1996.

[17] For example, the 1991 National Security Education Act (P.L. 102-183), the 1993 Government Performance and Results Act (P.L. 103-62), and the Congressional Report of the Commission on the Roles and Capabilities of the U.S. Intelligence Community, *Preparing for the 21st Century: An Appraisal of U.S. Intelligence* (Washington, DC: GPO, 1 March 1996), 87.

national security apparatus, this intelligence primer will shed light on why and how the government spends federal tax dollars on national intelligence.

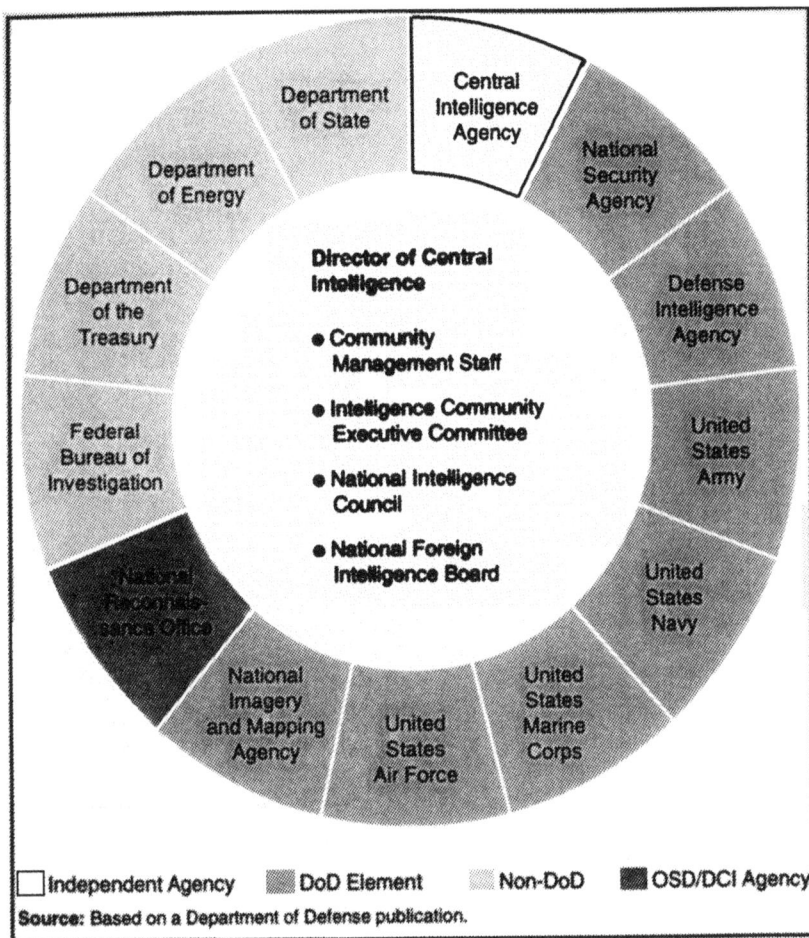

Figure 1: The National Intelligence Community.

PART I
INTELLIGENCE PROCESS

[I]ntelligence is more than information. It is knowledge that has been specially prepared for a customer's unique circumstances. The word *knowledge* highlights the need for human involvement. Intelligence collection systems produce... data, not intelligence; only the human mind can provide that special touch that makes sense of data for different customers' requirements. The special processing that partially defines intelligence is the continual collection, verification, and analysis of information that allows us to understand the problem or situation in actionable terms and then tailor a product in the context of the customer's circumstances. If any of these essential attributes is missing, then the product remains information rather than intelligence.[18]

The intelligence profession, already well established within government, is growing in the private sector. Intelligence is traditionally a function of government organizations serving the decisionmaking needs of national security authorities. But innovative private firms are increasingly adapting the national security intelligence model to the business world to aid their own strategic planning. Although business professionals may prefer the term "information" over "intelligence," the author will use the latter term to highlight the importance of adding value to information. According to government convention, the author will use the term "customer" to refer to the intended recipient of an intelligence product — either a fellow intelligence service member, or a policy official or decisionmaker. The process of converting raw information into actionable intelligence can serve government and business equally well in their respective domains.

The Intelligence Process in Government and Business

Production of intelligence follows a cyclical *process*, a series of repeated and interrelated steps that add value to original inputs and create a substantially transformed product. That transformation is what distinguishes intelligence from a simple cyclical activity.[19] In government and private sector alike, analysis is the catalyst that converts information into intelligence for planners and decisionmakers.

Although the intelligence process is complex and dynamic, several component functions may be distinguished from the whole. In this primer, components are identified as Intelligence Needs, Collection Activities, Processing of Collected Information, Analysis and Production. To highlight the components, each is accorded a separate Part in this study. These

---

[18] Captain William S. Brei, *Getting Intelligence Right The Power of Logical Procedure*, Occasional Paper Number Two (Washington, DC: Joint Military Intelligence College, January 1996), 4.

[19] Melissie C Rumizen, Benchmarking Manager at the National Security Agency, interview by author, 4 January 1996

labels, and the illustration below, should not be interpreted to mean that intelligence is a uni dimensional and unidirectional process. "[I]n fact, the [process] is multidimensional, multi directional, and — most importantly — interactive and iterative."[20]

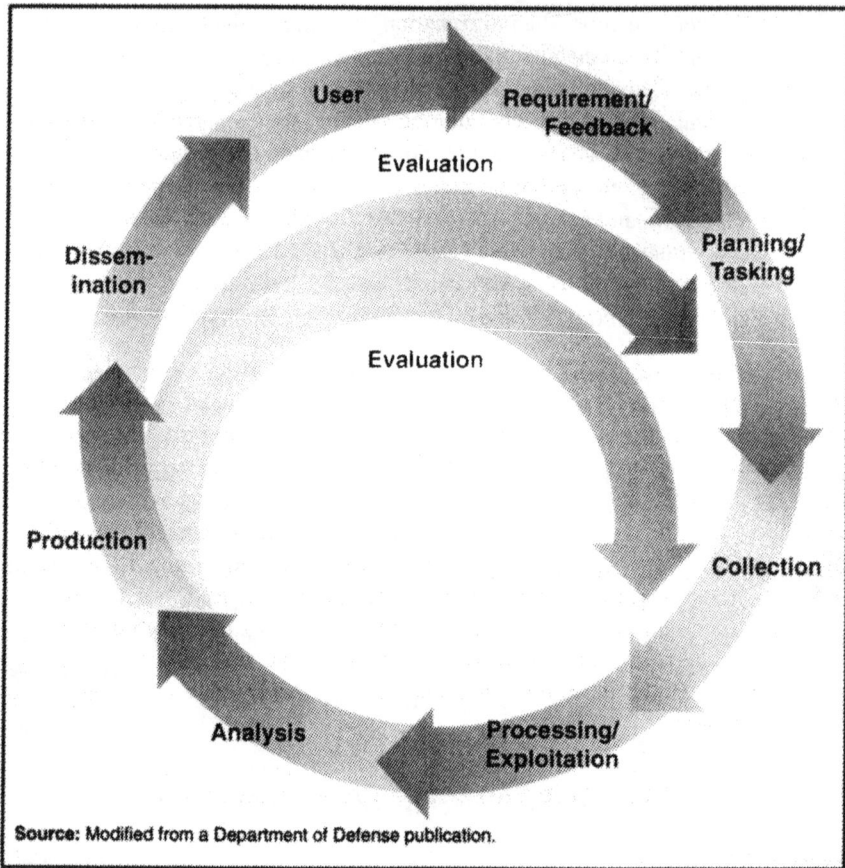

Source: Modified from a Department of Defense publication.

Figure 2: Process of Intelligence Creation and Use.

[20] Douglas H Dearth, "National Intelligence: Profession and Process," in *Strategic Intelligence: Theory and Application*, eds Douglas H. Dearth and R Thomas Goodden, 2d ed. (Washington, DC. Joint Military Intelligence Training Center, 1995), 17.

The purpose of this process is for the intelligence service to provide decisionmakers with tools, or "products" that assist them in identifying key decision factors. Such intelligence products may be described both in terms of their subject content and their intended use.[21]

Table 1: Types of Intelligence Product Categories
Source: adapted from Garst, "Components of Intelligence"

By Subject	By Use
Biographic	Research
Economic	Current
Geographic	Estimative
Military	Operational
Political	Scientific and Technical
Sociological	Warning
Scientific and Technical	
Transportation and Communications	

Any or all of these categories may be relevant to the private sector, depending upon the particular firm's product line and objectives in a given industry, market environment, and geographic area.

A nation's power or a firm's success results from a combination of factors, so intelligence producers and customers should examine potential adversaries and competitive situations from as many relevant viewpoints as possible. A competitor's economic resources, political alignments, the number, education and health of its people, and apparent objectives are all important in determining the ability of a country or a business to exert influence on others. The eight subject categories of intelligence are exhaustive, but they are not mutually exclusive. Although dividing intelligence into subject areas is useful for analyzing information and administering production, it should not become a rigid formula. Some intelligence services structure production into geographic subject areas when their responsibilities warrant a broader perspective than topical divisions would allow.[22]

---

[21] Ronald D Garst, "Components of Intelligence," in *A Handbook of Intelligence Analysis*, ed Ronald D Garst, 2d ed (Washington, DC: Defense Intelligence College, January 1989), 1, Central Intelligence Agency, *A Consumer's Guide to Intelligence* (Washington, DC: Public Affairs Staff, July 1995), 5-7.

[22] Garst, *Components of Intelligence*, 2,3.

Similarly, characterization of intelligence by intended use applies to both government and enterprise, and the categories again are exhaustive, but not mutually exclusive. The production of basic research intelligence yields structured summaries of topics such as geographic, demographic, and political studies, presented in handbooks, charts, maps, and the like. Current intelligence addresses day-to-day events to apprise decisionmakers of new developments and assess their significance. Estimative intelligence deals with what might be or what might happen; it may help policymakers fill in gaps between available facts, or assess the range and likelihood of possible outcomes in a threat or "opportunity" scenario. Operational support intelligence incorporates all types of intelligence by use, but is produced in a tailored, focused, and timely manner for planners and operators of the supported activity. Scientific and Technical intelligence typically comes to life in in-depth, focused assessments stemming from detailed physical or functional examination of objects, events, or processes, such as equipment manufacturing techniques.[23] Warning intelligence sounds an alarm, connoting urgency, and implies the potential need for policy action in response.

How government and business leaders define their needs for these types of intelligence affects the intelligence service's organization and operating procedures. Managers of this intricate process, whether in government or business, need to decide whether to make one intelligence unit responsible for all the component parts of the process or to create several specialized organizations for particular sub-processes. This question is explored briefly below, and more fully in Part VII.

Functional Organization of Intelligence

The national Intelligence Community comprises Executive Branch agencies that produce classified and unclassified studies on selected foreign developments as a prelude to decisions and actions by the president, military leaders, and other senior authorities. Some of this intelligence is developed from special sources to which few individuals have access except on a strictly controlled "need-to-know" basis.[24] The four categories of special intelligence are Human Resources (HUMINT), Signals (SIGINT), Imagery (IMINT) and Measurement and Signatures (MASINT). The four corresponding national authorities for these categories are the Central Intelligence Agency (CIA), the National Security Agency (NSA), the National Imagery and Mapping Agency (NIMA) and the Defense Intelligence Agency (DIA). DIA shares authority for HUMINT, being responsible for Department of Defense HUMINT management. Along with these four agencies, other members of the Intelligence Community use and produce intelligence by integrating all available and relevant collected information into reports tailored to the needs of individual customers.

Private sector organizations use open-source information to produce intelligence in a fashion similar to national authorities. By mimicking the government process of translating customer needs into production requirements, and particularly by performing rigorous analysis on gathered information, private organizations can produce assessments that aid their leaders in

---

[23] CIA, *Consumer's Guide*, 5-7
[24] CIA, *Consumer's Guide*, vii

planning and carrying out decisions to increase their competitiveness in the global economy. This primer will point out why private entities may desire to transfer into their domain some well-honed proficiencies developed in the national Intelligence Community. At the same time, the Intelligence Community self-examination conducted in these pages may allow government managers to reflect on any unique capabilities worthy of further development and protection.

Human Source Intelligence (HUMINT)

- Agents *(Controlled Sources)*
- Informants *(Willing Sources)*
- Observers *(Attaches)*

Imagery Intelligence (IMINT)

- Photo/Digital
- Electro-Optical
- Multispectral
- Infrared
- Radar

Open Source Intelligence (OSINT)

- Public Documents
- Newspapers
- Television and Radio
- Books and Journals

Signals Intelligence

- COMINT *(Communications)*
- ELINT *(Electronic)*
- FISINT *(Telemetry)*

Measurement and Signatures Intelligence (MASINT)

- ACINT *(Acoustic)*
- RADINT *(Radiation)*

Source: Modified from a Department of Defense publication

Figure 3: National Intelligence Production Resources.

PART II
CONVERTING CUSTOMER NEEDS INTO
INTELLIGENCE REQUIREMENTS

The articulation of the requirement is the most important part of the process, and it seldom is as simple as it might seem. There should be a dialogue concerning the requirement, rather than a simple assertion of need. Perhaps the customer knows precisely what is needed and what the product should look like. Perhaps... not. Interaction is required: discussion between ultimate user and principal producer. This is often difficult due to time, distance, and bureaucratic impediments, not to mention disparities of rank, personality, perspectives, and functions.[25]

Defining the Intelligence Problem

Customer demands, or "needs," particularly if they are complex and time-sensitive, require interpretation or analysis by the intelligence service before being expressed as intelligence requirements that drive the production process.[26] This dialog between intelligence producer and customer may begin with a simple set of questions, and if appropriate, progress to a more sophisticated analysis of the intelligence problem being addressed.

The "Five Ws" — *Who, What, When, Where,* and *Why* — are a good starting point for translating intelligence needs into requirements. A sixth related question, *How*, may also be considered. In both government and business, these questions form the basic framework for decisionmakers and intelligence practitioners to follow in formulating intelligence requirements and devising a strategy to satisfy them. Typically, government intelligence requirements are expressed in terms of foreign threats to national or international security. In business, requirements may be expressed in terms of the competitor's standing in the marketplace in comparison to one's own posture. Representative examples from each sector follow:

---

[25] Dearth, "National Intelligence," 17-18.
[26] Dearth, "National Intelligence," 18.

Table 2: Illustrative Definitions of Intelligence Problems and Customer Needs
Source: Author

A Government Scenario

The Intelligence Problem

Who	What	When	Where	Why	How
A foreign president	Refusing to allow weapons sites to be inspected	Now; for several months	Country X	Unknown, possibly to hide illegal weapons	Barring access, destroying monitoring equipment

The Intelligence Need

Who	What	When	Where	Why	How
U.S. President	Wants info on Country X President	Now, and update	White House	Determine power base and intent	All-source collection & analysis

A Business Scenario

The Intelligence Problem

Who	What	When	Where	Why	How
Company X	Reorganizes production department	Sudden	Saturated market	Unknown	Unknown

The Intelligence Need

Who	What	When	Where	Why	How
CEO of similar Company Y	Wants to know why and how Company X changed	ASAP	CEO's office	Determine if new structure gives advantage	Open source analysis; tailored, confidential report

Examination of these basic scenarios should inspire further development of the concept of determining customer needs in specific situations. The thoughtful researcher may propose, for example, ways to gather information on additional aspects of the problem (Who, What) and on customers (Who), as well as on the attendant motivations (Why) and strategies (How) of the target and the customer. Defining the intelligence problem in this manner paves the way for the next step in the intelligence process — the development of intelligence collection, analysis, and production *requirements*, explained later in this chapter.

Another, more complex model for defining intelligence scenarios employs the Taxonomy of Problem Types.[27] The table below illustrates the factors that customers and producers may take into account in articulating the nature of the intelligence problem and selecting a strategy for resolving it.

Table 3: Taxonomy of Problem Types

Source: Analysis course material, Joint Military Intelligence College, 1991

Characteristics	Problem Types				
	Simplistic	Deterministic	Moderately Random	Severely Random	Indeterminate
What is the question?	Obtain information	How much? How many	Identify and rank all outcomes	Identify outcomes in unbounded situation	Predict future events/ situations
Role of facts	Highest	High	Moderate	Low	Lowest
Role of judgment	Lowest	Low	Moderate	High	Highest
Analytical task	Find information	Find/create formula	Generate all outcomes	Define potential outcomes	Define futures factors
Analytical method	Search sources	Match data to formula	Decision theory; utility analysis	Role playing and gaming	Analyze models and scenarios
Analytical instrument	Matching	Mathematical formula	Influence diagram, utility, probability	Subjective evaluation of outcomes	Use of experts
Analytic output	Fact	Specific value or number	Weighted alternative outcomes	Plausible outcomes	Elaboration on expected future
Probability of error	Lowest	Very low	Dependent on data quality	High to very high	Highest
Follow-up task	None	None	Monitor for change	Repeated testing to determine true state	Exhaustive learning

---

[27] Morgan D. Jones, *The Thinker's Toolkit* (New York: Random House, 1995), 44-46, as elaborated by Thomas H. Murray, Sequoia Associates, Inc., Arlington, VA., in coursework at the Joint Military Intelligence College.

As with the "Five Ws," this model enables decisionmakers and analysts to assess their needs and capabilities in relation to a particular intelligence scenario. This ability to establish a baseline and set in motion a collection and production strategy is crucial to conducting a successful intelligence effort. Too often, both producers and customers waste valuable time and effort struggling to characterize for themselves a given situation, or perhaps worse, they hastily embark upon an action plan without determining its appropriateness to the problem. Employing a structured approach as outlined in the Taxonomy of Problem Types can help the players avoid these inefficiencies and take the first step toward generating clear intelligence requirements by defining both the intelligence problem and the requisite components to its solution. Following are example scenarios. The reader is encouraged to follow the scenarios down the columns of the taxonomy table, then generate new scenarios in similar fashion.

Intelligence Problem Definition

A Government Scenario

The Severely Random problem type is one frequently encountered by the military in planning an operational strategy. This is the realm of wargaming. The initial intelligence problem is to identify all possible outcomes in an unbounded situation, so that commanders can generate plans for every contingency. The role of valid data is relatively minor, while the role of judgment is great, as history and current statistics may shed little light on how the adversary will behave in a hypothetical situation, and the progress and outcome of an operation against that adversary cannot be predicted with absolute accuracy. Therefore, the analytical task is to define and prepare for all potential outcomes. The analytical method is role playing and wargaming: placing oneself mentally in the imagined situation, and experiencing it in advance, even to the point of acting it out in a realistic setting. After experiencing the various scenarios, the players subjectively evaluate the outcomes of the games, assessing which ones may be plausible or expected to occur in the real world. The probability of error in judgment here is inherently high, as no one can be certain that the future will occur exactly as events unfolded in the game. However, repeated exercises can help to establish a measure of confidence, for practice in living out these scenarios may enable the players to more quickly identify and execute desired behaviors, and avoid mistakes in a similar real situation.

A Business Scenario

The Indeterminate problem type is one facing the entrepreneur in the modern telecommunications market. Predicting the future for a given proposed new technology or product is an extremely imprecise task fraught with potentially dire, or rewarding, consequences. The role of valid data is extremely minor here, whereas analytical judgments about the buying public's future — and changing — needs and desires are crucial. Defining the key factors influencing the future market is the analytical task, to be approached via the analytical method of setting up models and scenarios: the if/then/else process. Experts in the proposed technology or market are then employed to analyze these possibilities. Their output is a synthesized assessment of how the future will look under various conditions with regard to the proposed new product. The probability of error in judgment is extremely high, as the decision is based entirely on mental models rather than experience; after all, neither the new product nor the future environment exists yet. Continual reassessment of the changing factors influencing the future can help the analysts adjust their conclusions and better advise decisionmakers on whether, and how, to proceed with the new product.

Generating Intelligence Requirements

Once they have agreed upon the nature of the intelligence problem at hand, the intelligence service and the customer together can next generate intelligence *requirements* to drive the production process. The intelligence requirement translates customer needs into an intelligence action plan. A good working relationship between the two parties at this stage will determine whether the intelligence produced in subsequent stages actually meets customer needs. However, the differing perspectives that each side brings to the negotiation process can make cooperation between them a difficult feat.[28]

Customers want intelligence to guide them clearly in making policy and operational decisions. They may have little understanding of the intelligence process, and little patience for the subjectivity and conditionality of intelligence judgments. For customers, intelligence can be just one of many influences on their decisionmaking, and may be given little weight in comparison to other, more readily digested, familiar, or policy-oriented inputs. However, intelligence is neither designed nor equipped to meet these customer expectations.[29]

As a discipline, intelligence seeks to remain an independent, objective advisor to the decisionmaker. The realm of intelligence is that of "fact," considered judgment, and probability, but not prescription. It does not tell the customer what to do to meet an agenda, but rather, identifies the factors at play, and how various actions may affect outcomes. Intelligence tends to be packaged in standard formats and, because of its methodical approach, may not be delivered within the user's ideal timeframe. For all these reasons, the customer may not see intelligence as a useful service.[30]

Yet, somehow the intelligence producer and customer must reconcile their differing perspectives in order to agree on intelligence requirements and make the production process work. Understanding each other's views on intelligence is the first step toward improving the relationship between them. The next step is communication. Free interaction among the players will foster agreement on intelligence priorities and result in products that decisionmakers recognize as meaningful to their agendas, yet balanced by rigorous analysis.[31] In addition, as discussed below, customer feedback on production quality will lead to better definition of future intelligence problems and requirements.

---

[28] Arthur S. Hulnick, "The Intelligence Producer-Policy Consumer Linkage: A Theoretical Approach," *Intelligence and National Security*, 1, No. 2, (May 1986): 214-216.

[29] Hulnick, "Producer-Policy Consumer Linkage," 215-216.

[30] Hulnick, "Producer-Policy Consumer Linkage," 216.

[31] Adapted from Michael A. Turner, "Setting Analytical Priorities in U.S. Intelligence," *International Journal of Intelligence and CounterIntelligence*, 9, No. 3, (Fall 1996): 320-322.

Types of Intelligence Requirements

Having thus developed an understanding of customer needs, the intelligence service may proactively and continuously generate intelligence collection and production requirements to maintain customer-focused operations. Examples of such internally generated specifications include analyst-driven, events-driven, and scheduled requirements. The table below briefly describes them.[32]

Table 4: Types of Producer-Generated Intelligence Collection and Production Requirements

Source: Hulnick

Analyst-driven	Based on knowledge of customer and issues
Events-driven	In response to time-sensitive relevant events
Scheduled	Periodic activities to document and update target status

Further distinctions among intelligence requirements include timeliness and scope, or level, of intended use. Timeliness of requirements is established to meet standing (long-term) and *ad hoc* (short-term) needs. When the customer and intelligence service agree to define certain topics as long-term intelligence issues, they generate a standing requirement to ensure that a regular production effort can, and will, be maintained against that target. The customer will initiate an *ad hoc* requirement upon realizing a sudden short-term need for a specific type of intelligence, and will specify the target of interest, the coverage timeframe, and the type of output desired.

The scope or level of intended use of the intelligence may be characterized as strategic or tactical. Strategic intelligence is geared to a policymaker dealing with big-picture issues affecting the mission and future of an organization: the U.S. President, corporate executives, high-level diplomats, or military commanders of major commands or fleets. Tactical intelligence serves players and decisionmakers "on the ground" engaged in current operations: trade negotiators, marketing and sales representatives, deployed military units, or product developers.

Table 5: Types of Customer-Defined Intelligence Requirements

Source: Author

Timeliness	Short-term *(ad hoc)*	Long-term (standing)
Scope	Broad (strategic)	Narrow (tactical)

---

[32] Adapted from Arthur S. Hulnick, "Managing Intelligence Analysis: Strategies for Playing the End Game," *International Journal of Intelligence and CounterIntelligence* 2, No. 3 (Fall 1988): 327.

Ensuring that Requirements Meet Customer Needs

Even when they follow this method of formulating intelligence requirements together, decisionmakers and their intelligence units in the public and private sectors may still have an incomplete grasp of how to define their needs and capabilities — until they have evaluated the resultant products. Thus, customer feedback, production planning and tasking, as well as any internal product evaluation, all become part of the process of defining needs and creating intelligence requirements. However, when intelligence producers and users are not in nearly direct, daily contact, this process can consume a good deal of time. This is why the national Intelligence Community is experimenting with compressing both the accustomed time and spatial dimensions of the intelligence process through remote electronic collaboration and production methods.[33]

Whether in business or government, six fundamental values or attributes underlie the core principles from which all the essential intelligence functions are derived. The corollary is that intelligence customers' needs may be defined and engaged by intelligence professionals using these same values. Table 6 offers a brief explanation of how both intelligence customers and producers may use these values to evaluate how well they have translated needs into requirements that will result in useful products.[34]

Interpretation of these values turns a customer's need into a collection and production requirement that the intelligence service understands in the context of its own functions. However, illustrating the complexity of the intelligence process, once this is done, the next step is not necessarily collection.

Rather, the next stage is analysis. Perhaps the requirement is simply and readily answered — by an existing product, by ready extrapolation from files or data bases, or by a simple phone call or short desk note based on an analyst's or manager's knowledge. On the other hand, the requirement might necessitate laborious effort — extrapolation, collation, analysis, integration, and production — but still the product can be constructed and sent directly to the requester. Case closed; next problem.... Preliminary analysis might well show, however, that while much data exists, because the issue at hand is not a new one, gaps in information must be filled... Obviously, this calls for collection. This brings up an essential point: consumers do not drive collection *per se*; analysts do — or should.[35] Part III explores this next step in the intelligence process.

---

[33] The U.S. military has pioneered the concept of an electronic intelligence operating environment that transcends organizational boundaries. Congress has recommended that the IC adopt this *Joint Intelligence Virtual Architecture* model to take advantage of technological developments, reduce bureaucratic barriers, and thereby provide policymakers with timely, objective, and useful intelligence. See U.S. Congress Staff Study, House Permanent Select Committee on Intelligence, *IC21: The Intelligence Community in the 21st Century*, (April 1996): Section III, "Intelligence Requirements Process."

[34] The six values are adapted by Brei from an earlier version of U.S. Department of Defense, Joint Chiefs of Staff, Joint Pub 2-0, *Joint Doctrine for Intelligence Support to Operations* (Washington, DC: GPO, 5 May 1995), IV-15.

[35] Dearth, "National Intelligence," 18-19.

Table 6: Intelligence Values

Source: Brei

Accuracy: All sources and data must be evaluated for the possibility of technical error, misperception, and hostile efforts to mislead.

Objectivity: All judgments must be evaluated for the possibility of deliberate distortions and manipulations due to self-interest.

Usability: All intelligence communications must be in a form that facilitates ready comprehension and immediate application. Intelligence products must be compatible with a customer's capabilities for receiving, manipulating, protecting, and storing the product.

Relevance: Information must be selected and organized for its applicability to a customer's requirements, with potential consequences and significance of the information made explicit to the customer's circumstances.

Readiness: Intelligence systems must be responsive to the existing and contingent intelligence requirements of customers at all levels of command.

Timeliness: Intelligence must be delivered while the content is still actionable under the customer's circumstances.

PART III
COLLECTION

The collection function rests on research — on matching validated intelligence objectives to available sources of information, with the results to be transformed into usable intelligence. Just as within needs-definition, analysis is an integral function of collection.

Collection Requirements

The collection *requirement* specifies exactly how the intelligence service will go about acquiring the intelligence information the customer needs. Any one, or any of several, players in the intelligence system may be involved in formulating collection requirements: the intelligence analyst, a dedicated staff officer, or a specialized collection unit.

In large intelligence services, collection requirements may be managed by a group of specialists acting as liaisons between customers and collectors (people who actually obtain the needed information, either directly or by use of technical means). Within that requirements staff, individual requirements officers may be dedicated to a particular set of customers, a type of collection resource, or a specific intelligence issue. This use of collection requirements officers is prevalent in the government. Smaller services, especially in the private sector, may assign collection requirements management to one person or team within a multidisciplinary intelligence unit that serves a particular customer or that is arrayed against a particular topic area.

Regardless of how it is organized, the requirements management function entails much more than simple administrative duties. It requires analytic skill to evaluate how well the customer has expressed the intelligence need; whether, how and when the intelligence unit is able to obtain the required information through its available collection sources; and in what form to deliver the collected information to the intelligence analyst.

Collection Planning and Operations

One method for selecting a collection strategy is to first prepare a list of expected target evidence. The collection requirements officer and the intelligence analyst for the target may collaborate in identifying the most revealing evidence of target activity, which may include physical features of terrain or objects, human behavior, or natural and manmade phenomena. The issue that can be resolved through this analysis is "What am I looking for, and how will I know it if I see it"?

Successful analysis of expected target evidence in light of the customer's needs can determine what collection source and method will permit detection and capture of that evidence. Increasingly sophisticated identification of evidence types may reveal what collectible data are essential for drawing key conclusions, and therefore should be given priority; whether the evidence is distinguishable from innocuous information; and whether the intelligence service has the skills, time, money and authorization to collect the data needed to exploit a particular target. Furthermore, the collection must yield information in a format that is either usable in raw form by the intelligence analyst, or that can be converted practicably into usable form.

For example, in the case of the first business scenario presented in Part II, the CEO needs intelligence on why and how the similar, competitor company suddenly reorganized its production department. The collection requirement might specify that the intelligence unit give first priority to this new issue; it will focus on collecting information about the competitor's reorganization. A list of relevant evidence might include the following: changes in personnel assignments, changes in supply of production components, budget deficit or surplus, age of infrastructure, breakthroughs in research and development, and changes in the cultural or natural environment. To exploit this evidence, the intelligence service would thus need direct or indirect access to information on the company's employees, its previous production methods, its financial status, its physical plant, its overall functional structure and operations, and the consumer market. The collection unit would choose from among the sources listed in Table 7 below those most likely to provide timely access to this information in usable form.

Finally, upon defining the collection requirement and selecting a collection strategy, the intelligence unit should implement that strategy by tasking personnel and resources to exploit selected sources, perform the collection, re-format the results if necessary to make them usable in the next stages, and forward the information to the intelligence production unit. This aspect of the collection phase may be called collection operations management. As with requirements management, it is often done by specialists, particularly in the large intelligence service. In smaller operations, the same person or team may perform some or all of the collection-related functions.

The small, multidisciplinary intelligence unit may experience certain benefits and disadvantages in managing multiple phases of the intelligence process at the same time. In comparison to the large, compartmentalized service, the smaller unit will likely experience greater overall efficiency of operations and fewer bureaucratic barriers to customer service. The same few people may act as requirements officers, operations managers and intelligence analysts/producers, decreasing the likelihood of communication and scheduling problems among them. This approach may be less expensive in terms of infrastructure and logistics than a functionally divided operation. On the other hand, the financial and time investment in training each individual in every facet of the intelligence process may be substantial. Furthermore, careful selection and assignment of personnel who thrive in a multidisciplinary environment will be vital to the unit's success, to help ward off potential worker stress and overload. An additional pitfall that the small unit should strive to avoid is the tendency to be self-limiting: overreliance on the same customer contacts, collection sources and methods, analytic approaches, and production formulas can lead to stagnation and irrelevance. The small intelligence unit should be careful to invest in new initiatives that keep pace with changing times and customer needs.

Collection Sources

The range of sources available to all intelligence analysts, including those outside of government, is of course much broader than the set of restricted, special sources available only for government use. U.S. government collection of information for intelligence purposes is channelled through the recognized intelligence collection disciplines described in Part I. From a different perspective, four general categories serve to identify the types of information sources available to the intelligence analyst: people, objects, emanations, and records. Strictly speaking, the information offered by these sources may not be called intelligence if the information has not yet been converted into a value-added product. In the government or private sector, collection may be performed by the reporting analyst or by a specialist in one or more of the collection disciplines. The following table, derived from Clauser and Weir, illustrates the distinct attributes offered by the four sources of intelligence.[36]

Table 7: Categories of Intelligence Sources by Analytic Use

Source: Adapted from Clauser and Weir

Source	Related Collection Discipline(s) and Source Attributes	Analytic Use
People	HUMINT; subject-matter experts, professional researchers, information specialists, eyewitnesses or participants	Transfer of first-hand knowledge, referral to other sources
Objects	IMINT; physical characteristics of equipment, materials, or products, such as texture, shape, size, and distinctive markings	Basis for emotive but objective reporting on composition, condition, origin, or human purpose
Emanations	MASINT, SIGINT; detectable phenomena given off by natural or man-made objects; electromagnetic energy, heat, sound, footprints, fingerprints, and chemical and material residues	Scientific and technical analysis
Records	IMINT, SIGINT, symbolic (written and oral reports, numerical tabulations) or non-symbolic (images, electro-magnetic recordings of data)	Research, background information, translation, conversion to usable form

---

[36] Jerome K. Clauser and Sandra M. Weir, *Intelligence Research Methodology: An Introduction to Techniques and Procedures for Conducting Research in Defense Intelligence* (Washington, DC: Defense Intelligence School, 1975), 111-117.

The following table offers examples from government and business of each source type.

Table 8: Comparison of Illustrative Intelligence Sources from Government and Business

Source: Author

Source	Information Provided	Government	Business
People	Inadvertent or intentional revelation by a person in a casual encounter, official meeting, or informant relationship	A foreign diplomat	A fellow exhibitor at a trade show
Objects	Physical and functional characteristics of the item, discerned through physical or visual examination	Military equipment	Products or components
Emanations	Clues about the identity and activities of the originator	Intercepted communications	Trace chemicals in factory effluent
Records	Evidence of existence and characteristics of target entities	Imagery, telemetry, documents	Product literature

The collection phase of the intelligence process thus involves several steps: translation of the intelligence need into a collection requirement, definition of a collection strategy, selection of collection sources, and information collection. The resultant collected information must often undergo a further conversion before it can yield intelligence in the analysis stage. Processing of collected information into intelligence information is addressed in the following Part of this primer.

PART IV
PROCESSING COLLECTED
INFORMATION

From Raw Data to Intelligence Information

No matter what the setting or type of collection, gathered information must be packaged meaningfully before it can be used in the production of intelligence. Processing methods will vary depending on the form of the collected information and its intended use, but they include everything done to make the results of collection efforts usable by intelligence producers. Typically, "processing" applies to the techniques used by government intelligence services to transform raw data from special-source technical collection into intelligence *information*.[37]

> While collectors collect "raw" information, certain [collection] disciplines involve a sort of *pre-analysis* in order to make the information "readable" to the average all-source analyst. For instance: imagery analysts "read-out" the basic information on the image; foreign language broadcasts must be literally translated by linguists and analyzed for linguistic "context"; electronic signals require sorting out to be intelligible to the uninitiated in that arcane art; agent reports also need literal translations and perhaps comments as to access, context, assumed or proven past veracity.[38]

In the private sector, some processing activities are analogous to those of the government. Interpreting and annotating open-source information for a business intelligence service may include: marking locations of interest on a map or photograph, "translating" press releases or technical reports, transcribing the words of a speaker from video or audiotape into text, or drafting a detailed commentary from a personal interview.

Another term for processing, *collation*, encompasses many of the different operations that must be performed on collected information or data before further analysis and intelligence production can occur. More than merely physically manipulating information, collation organizes the information into a usable form, adding meaning where it was not evident in the original. Collation includes gathering, arranging, and annotating related information; drawing tentative conclusions about the relationship of "facts" to each other and their significance; evaluating the accuracy and reliability of each item; grouping items into logical categories; critically examining the information source; and assessing the meaning and usefulness of the content for further analysis. Collation reveals information

---

[37] The Department of Defense defines intelligence information as "unprocessed data of every description which may be used in the production of intelligence." (Department of Defense, Joint Chiefs of Staff, Joint Pub 1-02, *Dictionary of Military and Associated Terms* (Washington, DC: 23 March 1994), 184.)

[38] Dearth, "National Intelligence," 19.

gaps, guides further collection and analysis, and provides a framework for selecting and organizing additional information.[39]

Examples of collation include filing documents, condensing information by categories or relationships, and employing electronic database programs to store, sort, and arrange large quantities of information or data in preconceived or self-generating patterns. Regardless of its form or setting, an effective collation method will have the following attributes:

1. Be impersonal. It should not depend on the memory of one analyst; another person knowledgeable in the subject should be able to carry out the operation.

2. Not become the "master" of the analyst or an end in itself.

3. Be free of bias in integrating the information.

4. Be receptive to new data without extensive alteration of the collating criterion.[40]

Evaluating and Selecting Evidence

To prepare collected information for further use, one must evaluate its relevance and value to the specific problem at hand. An examination of the information's *source* and *applicability* to the intelligence issue can determine whether that information will be further employed in the intelligence production process. Three aspects to consider in evaluating the relevance of information sources are reliability, proximity, and appropriateness.

Reliability of a source is determined through an evaluation of its past performance; if the source proved accurate in the past, then a reasonable estimate of its likely accuracy in a given case can be made. A human source's own testimony of reliability may also be taken into account; qualifiers such as "certain," "believe," and "guess" indicate how sure the source is of the information being conveyed. However, if the source is completely untested, then evaluation of the information must be done solely on its own merits, independent of its origin.[41]

Proximity refers to the source's closeness to the information. The direct observer or participant in an event may gather and present evidence directly, but in the absence of such firsthand information, the analyst must rely on sources with varying degrees of proximity to

---

[39] R.H. Mathams, "The Intelligence Analyst's Notebook," in *Strategic Intelligence: Theory and Application*, eds. Douglas H. Dearth and R. Thomas Goodden, 2d ed. (Washington, DC: Joint Military Intelligence Training Center, 1995), 85-86.

[40] Mathams, 86.

[41] adapted from Gary Harris, "Evaluating Intelligence Evidence," in *A Handbook of Intelligence Analysis*, ed Ronald D. Garst, 2d ed. (Washington, DC: Defense Intelligence College, January 1989), 34-35. For an in-depth treatment of evidence evaluation techniques and factors, see David A. Schum, *Evidence and Inference for the Intelligence Analyst*, Vols. I and II (Lanham, MD: University Press of America, 1987).

the situation. A primary source passes direct knowledge of an event on to the analyst. A secondary source provides information twice removed from the original event; one observer informs another, who then relays the account to the analyst. Such regression of source proximity may continue indefinitely, and naturally, the more numerous the steps between the information and the source, the greater the opportunity for error or distortion.[42]

Appropriateness of the source rests upon whether the source speaks from a position of authority on the specific issue in question. As no one person or institution is an expert on all matters, the source's individual capabilities and shortcomings affect the level of validity or reliability assigned to the information it provides regarding a given topic.[43]

The following examples illustrate the use of reliability, proximity, and appropriateness to evaluate a source.

> The mail clerk at 3rd Army Headquarters told me that, according to the 1st Armored Division Supply Officer, the Division is being deployed to Site Y in three days.

The reliability of the mail clerk as a source (questionable), his proximity to the information (secondary), and the appropriateness of the Supply Officer as a source on the fact of deployment (uncertain), make this information of little value to the intelligence production process.

> A major national newspaper published an interview with the CEO of Big Company, quoting the CEO's announcement of a merger the company had just secretly concluded with Large Company.

The reliability of a major national newspaper as a source (good), its proximity to the information (secondary), and the appropriateness of the CEO as the source of the merger announcement (high) make this information of high value to intelligence production.

Three aspects of the information itself have a bearing on its applicability to intelligence issues: plausibility, expectability, and support. *Plausibility* refers to whether the information is true under any circumstances or only under certain conditions, either known or possible. *Expectability* is assessed in the context of the analyst's prior knowledge of the subject. *Support* for information exists when another piece of evidence corroborates it — either the same information from a different source, or different information that points to the same conclusion.[44]

For example, a source contends that the President of Country X recently died, but the death is being kept secret from all but a few members of his regime. Although unusual, this information is plausible, and even has precedent in history. The scenario may meet the expectability criterion, if the country or this particular regime is known to be

---

[42] Harris, 35.
[43] adapted from Harris, 36.
[44] adapted from Harris, 36-38.

extremely secretive and paranoid about being vulnerable to hostile internal or external takeover movements. Support for this information may come from the same source providing details on the President's secret burial ceremony, or a different source, such as an actor who was hired to play the part of the President in a false Presidential address televised to the nation.

All these factors of source and content contribute to an initial assessment of the value of a particular piece of information to the intelligence production process. Those pieces that are judged to be useful may then undergo further scrutiny in light of customer needs, while items of questionable value may be rejected or set aside for further processing and comparison with other information. This initial selection of intelligence information sets the stage for intelligence analysis and production, as explained in the following Parts of the primer.

PART V
ANALYSIS

> Analysis is the breaking down of a large problem into a number of smaller problems and performing mental operations on the data in order to arrive at a conclusion or a generalization. It involves close examination of related items of information to determine the extent to which they confirm, supplement, or contradict each other and thus to establish probabilities and relationships.
>
> — *Mathams, 88.*

Analysis is not merely reorganizing data and information into a new format. At the very least, analysis should fully *describe* the phenomenon under study, accounting for as many relevant variables as possible. At the next higher level of analysis, a thorough *explanation* of the phenomenon is obtained, through interpreting the significance and effects of its elements on the whole. Ideally, analysis can reach successfully beyond the descriptive and explanatory levels to synthesis and effective persuasion, often referred to as *estimation.*

The *purpose* of intelligence analysis is to reveal to a specific decisionmaker the underlying significance of selected target information. Frequently intelligence analysis involves estimating the likelihood of one possible outcome, given the many possibilities in a particular scenario. This function is not to be confused with prediction, as no one can honestly be credited with predicting the future. However, intelligence analysis does appropriately involve forecasting, "which requires the explicit statement by the analyst of the degree of confidence held in a certain set of judgments, based upon a certain set of explicit facts or assumptions."[45] Different levels of analysis result in corresponding levels of conclusions that may be traced along an "Intelligence Food Chain."[46] This concept, illustrated in the following table, is equally applicable in government and business intelligence.

Table 9: The Intelligence Food Chain
Source: adapted from Davis, Analytic Tradecraft

Facts - verified information related to an intelligence issue (for example: events, measured characteristics).

Findings - expert knowledge based on organized information that indicates, for example, what is increasing, decreasing, changing, taking on a pattern.

Forecasts - judgments based on facts and findings and defended by sound and clear argumentation.

Fortunetelling - inadequately explained and defended judgments.

---

[45] Dearth, "National Intelligence," 25.

[46] Adapted from Jack Davis, *Intelligence Changes in Analytic Tradecraft in CIA's Directorate of Intelligence,* (Washington, DC: CIA Directorate of Intelligence, April 1995), 6.

Intelligence analysts may use this Food Chain model to measure their adherence to rigorous analytic thought — how far to go with their analytic judgments, and where to draw the line. The mnemonic "Four Fs Minus One" may serve as a reminder of how to apply this criterion. Whenever the intelligence information allows, and the customer's validated needs demand it, the intelligence analyst will extend the thought process as far along the Food Chain as possible, to the third "F" but not beyond to the fourth.

Types of Reasoning

Objectivity is the intelligence analyst's primary asset in creating intelligence that meets the Four Fs Minus One criterion. More than simply a conscientious attitude, objectivity is "a professional ethic that celebrates tough-mindedness and clarity in applying rules of evidence, inference, and judgment."[47] To produce intelligence objectively, the analyst must employ a process tailored to the nature of the problem. Four basic types of reasoning apply to intelligence analysis: induction, deduction, abduction and the scientific method.

Induction. The induction process is one of discovering relationships among the phenomena under study. For example, an analyst might discover from systematic examination of media reports that Country "X" had been issuing aggressive statements prior to formally announcing an arms agreement with Country "Y." Or an analyst may notice that a characteristic sequence of events always precedes Country "Z's" nuclear weapons tests.[48] In the words of Clauser and Weir:

> Induction is the intellectual process of drawing generalizations on the basis of observations or other evidence. Induction takes place when one learns from experience. For example, induction is the process by which a person learns to associate the color red with heat and heat with pain, and to generalize these associations to new situations.

> Induction occurs when one is able to postulate causal relationships. Intelligence estimates are largely the result of inductive processes, and, of course, induction takes place in the formulation of every hypothesis. Unlike other types of intellectual activities such as deductive logic and mathematics, there are no established rules for induction.[49]

Deduction. "Deduction is the process of reasoning from general rules to particular cases. Deduction may also involve drawing out or analyzing premises to form a conclusion."[50] In the case of Country "Z" above, the analyst noted a pattern of events related to testing of nuclear weapons. Later, after noticing this series of events occurring in Country "Z," the analyst may conclude that another nuclear weapons test is about to take place in that coun-

---

[47] Davis, *Analytical Tradecraft*, 5.
[48] Clauser and Weir, 81.
[49] Clauser and Weir, 81.
[50] clauser and Weir, 81.

try. The first premise, that certain events were related to weapons testing, was derived inductively — from specific observations to a conclusion. The second premise, that another test was imminent, was derived deductively — from a generalization to a specific case.[51]

Deduction works best in closed systems such as mathematics, formal logic, or certain kinds of games in which all the rules are clearly spelled out. For example, the validity and truthfulness of the following conclusion is apparent to anyone with a knowledge of geometry: "This is a triangle, therefore the sum of the interior angles will equal 180 degrees." In closed systems, properly drawn deductive conclusions are always valid.[52]

However, intelligence analysis rarely deals with closed systems, so premises assumed to be true may in fact be false, and lead to false conclusions. For example, in the weapons testing case above, Country "Z" may have deliberately deceived potential observers by falsely staging activities similar to those usually taken before a real weapons test. A conclusion that observed activities signalled a real test would be false in this case. Thus, as human activities rarely involve closed systems, deduction must be used carefully in intelligence analysis.[53]

Readers interested in further study into the use of deductive logic in estimative intelligence may wish to read the work of Israeli intelligence analyst Isaac Ben-Israel on this subject.[54] At the Joint Military Intelligence College, one student, Navy Lieutenant Donald Carney, explored the application of deductive logic to intelligence collection and analysis decisions in estimating the disintegration of Yugoslavia. Carney showed that Ben-Israel's "critical method" of inquiry could be applied prospectively to the collection of information to refute specific hypotheses, allowing for an unusually definitive estimate of the likelihood of each outcome.[55]

Abduction. Abduction is the process of generating a novel hypothesis to explain given evidence that does not readily suggest a familiar explanation. This process differs from induction in that it adds to the set of hypotheses available to the analyst. In inductive reasoning, the hypothesized relationship among pieces of evidence is considered to be already existing, needing only to be perceived and articulated by the analyst. In abduction, the analyst creatively generates an hypothesis, then sets about examining whether the available evidence unequivocally leads to the new conclusion. The latter step, testing the evidence, is a deductive inference.[56]

---

[51] Clauser and Weir, 82-83.

[52] Clauser and Weir, 83.

[53] Clauser and Weir, 83-84.

[54] Isaac Ben-Israel, "Philosophy and Methodology of Intelligence: The Logic of Estimative Process," *Intelligence and National Security 4*, no. 4 (October 1989): 660-718.

[55] LT Donald J. Carney, USN, *Estimating the Dissolution of Yugoslavia*, Seminar Paper (Washington, DC: Joint Military Intelligence College, September 1991).

[56] David A. Schum, *Evidence and Inference for the Intelligence Analyst*, Volume I (Lanham, MD: University Press of America, 1987): 20.

Abductive reasoning may also be called intuition, inspiration, or the "Ah-ha!" experience. It characterizes the analyst's occasional ability to come to a conclusion spontaneously, often without a sense of having consciously taken definable steps to get there. While the abduction process may not be easily defined or taught, it may be encouraged by providing analysts with a wide array of research material and experiences, and by supporting the expenditure of time and energy on creative thinking.[57]

Examples of abductive reasoning in intelligence analysis include situations in which the analyst has a nagging suspicion that something of intelligence value has happened or is about to happen, but has no immediate explanation for this conclusion. The government intelligence analyst may conclude that an obscure rebel faction in a target country is about to stage a political coup, although no overt preparations for the takeover are evident. The business analyst may determine that a competitor company is on the brink of a dramatic shift from its traditional product line into a new market, even though its balance sheet and status in the industry are secure. In each case, the analyst, trusting this sense that the time is right for a significant event, will set out to gather and evaluate evidence in light of the new, improbable, yet tantalizing hypothesis.

Scientific Method. The scientific method combines deductive and inductive reasoning: Induction is used to develop the hypothesis, and deduction is used to test it. In science, the analyst obtains data through direct observation of the subject and formulates an hypothesis to explain conclusions suggested by the evidence. Experiments on the subject are devised and conducted to test the validity of the hypothesis. If the experimental results match the expected outcome, then the hypothesis is validated; if not, then the analyst must develop a new hypothesis and appropriate experimental methods.[58]

In intelligence analysis, the analyst typically does not have direct access to the observable subject, but gathers information indirectly. From these gathered data, the intelligence analyst may proceed with the scientific method by generating tentative explanations for a subject event or phenomenon. Next, each hypothesis is examined for plausibility and compared against newly acquired information, in a continual process toward reaching a conclusion. Often the intelligence analyst tests several hypotheses at the same time, whereas the scientist usually focuses on one at a time. Furthermore, intelligence analysts cannot usually experiment directly upon the subject matter as in science, but must generate fictional scenarios and rigorously test them through mental processes such as those suggested below.[59]

---

[57] The relationship of this type of reasoning to Eastern philosophy is addressed in LCDR William G. Schmidlin, USN, *Zen and the Art of Intelligence Analysis*, MSSI Thesis (Washington, DC: Joint Military Intelligence College, July 1993).

[58] Mathams, 91. A seminal contribution to understanding scientific method is Abraham Kaplan's *The Conduct of Inquiry* (San Francisco, CA: Chandler, 1964). The applicability of this method in social science, and therefore, in intelligence, is developed in Earl Babbie's *The Practice of Social Research* (Belmont, CA: Wadsworth Publishing Co, 1992).

[59] Mathams, 91.

Methods of Analysis

Opportunity Analysis. Opportunity analysis identifies for policy officials opportunities or vulnerabilities that the customer's organization can exploit to advance a policy, as well as dangers that could undermine a policy.[60] It identifies institutions, interest groups, and key leaders in a target country or organization that support the intelligence customer's objective; the means of enhancing supportive elements; challenges to positive elements (which could be diminished or eliminated); logistic, financial, and other vulnerabilities of adversaries; and activities that could be employed to rally resources and support to the objective.[61] Jack Davis notes that in the conduct of opportunity analysis,

> [T]he analyst should start with the assumption that every policy concern can be transformed into a legitimate intelligence concern. What follows from this is that analysts and their managers should learn to think like a policymaker in order to identify the issues on which they can provide utility, but they should always [behave like intelligence producers]. ... The first step in producing effective opportunity analysis is to redefine an intelligence issue in the policymaker's terms. This requires close attention to the policymaker's role as "action officer" - reflecting a preoccupation with getting things started or stopped among adversaries and allies.... It also requires that analysts recognize a policy official's propensity to take risk for gain....[P]olicymakers often see, say, a one-in-five chance of turning a situation around as a sound investment of [organizational] prestige and their professional energies....[A]nalysts have to search for appropriate ways to help the policymaker inch the odds upward - not by distorting their bottom line when required to make a predictive judgment, or by cheerleading, but by pointing to opportunities as well as obstacles. Indeed, on politically sensitive issues, analysts would be well advised to utilize a matrix that first lists and then assesses both the promising and discouraging signs they, as objective observers, see for... policy goals.... [P]roperly executed opportunity analysis stresses information and possibilities rather than [explicit] predictions.[62]

Linchpin Analysis. Linchpin analysis is one way of showing intelligence managers and policy officials alike that all the bases have been touched. Linchpin analysis, a colorful term for structured forecasting, is an *anchoring* tool that seeks to reduce the hazard of self-inflicted intelligence error as well as policymaker misinterpretation. At a minimum, linchpin tradecraft promotes rigor through a series of predrafting checkpoints, outlined below. Analysts can also use it to organize and evaluate their text when addressing issues

---

[60] Jack Davis, *The Challenge of Opportunity Analysis* (Washington, DC: Center for the Study of Intelligence, July 1992), v.

[61] Davis, *Opportunity Analysis*, 7.

[62] Davis, *Opportunity Analysis*, 12-13.

of high uncertainty. Reviewing managers can use — and have used — linchpin standards to ensure that the argument in such assessments is sound and clear.[63]

Table 10: Steps in Linchpin Analysis
Source: Davis, *Analytic Tradecraft*

1. Identify the main uncertain factors or key variables judged likely to drive the outcome of the issue, forcing systematic attention to the range of and relationships among factors at play.

2. Determine the *linchpin* premises or working assumptions about the drivers. This encourages testing of the key subordinate judgments that hold the estimative conclusion together.

3. Marshal findings and reasoning in defense of the linchpins, as the premises that warrant the conclusion are subject to debate as well as error.

4. Address the circumstances under which unexpected developments could occur. What *indicators* or patterns of development could emerge to signal that the linchpins were unreliable? And what *triggers* or dramatic internal and external events could reverse the expected momentum?

Analogy. Analogies depend on the real or presumed similarities between two things. For example, analysts might reason that because two aircraft have many features in common, they may have been designed to perform similar missions. The strength of any such analogy depends upon the strength of the connection between a given condition and a specified result. In addition, the analyst must consider the characteristics that are dissimilar between the phenomena under study. The dissimilarities may be so great that they render the few similarities irrelevant.

> One of the most widely used tools in intelligence analysis is the analogy. Analogies serve as the basis for most hypotheses, and rightly or wrongly, underlie many generalizations about what the other side will do and how they will go about doing it.[64]

Thus, drawing well-considered generalizations is the key to using analogy effectively. When postulating human behavior, the analyst may effectively use analogy by applying it to a specific person acting in a situation similar to one in which his actions are well documented: an election campaign or a treaty negotiation, for example. However, an assumption that a different individual running for the same office or negotiating a similar treaty would behave the same way as his predecessor may be erroneous. The key condition in this analogy is the personality of the individual, not the similar situations. This principle of appropriate comparison applies equally to government and business intelligence analysis.

---

[63] Davis, *Analytic Tradecraft*, 8-9.
[64] Clauser and Weir, 246-248.

Analogies are used in many different kinds of intelligence analyses from military and political to industrial intelligence. For example, major U.S. auto makers purchase their competitors' models as soon as they appear in the showrooms. The new cars are taken to laboratories where they are completely and methodically disassembled. Reasoning by analogy, that is, assuming that it would cost one producer the same amount to produce or purchase the same components used by another, the major auto producers can estimate their competitors' per-unit production costs, any cost-saving measures taken, and how much profit is likely to be earned by the sale of a single unit.[65]

Customer Focus

As with the previous stages of the intelligence process, effective analysis depends upon a good working relationship between the intelligence customer and producer. A significant difference exists between the public and private sectors with regard to this customer-producer relationship. Government analysts typically benefit from close interaction with policymakers by virtue of their well understood institutional position. The same is not often true in the business world, where the intelligence analyst's role is not yet well institutionalized.

The government intelligence analyst is generally considered a legitimate and necessary policymaking resource, and even fairly junior employees may be accepted as national experts by virtue of the knowledge and analytic talent they offer to high level customers. Conversely, in the private sector, the intelligence analyst's corporate rank is generally orders of magnitude lower than that of a company vice-president or CEO. The individual analyst may have little access to the ultimate customer, and the intelligence service as a whole may receive little favor from a senior echelon that makes little distinction between so-called intelligence and the myriad of other decisionmaking inputs. When private sector practitioners apply validated methods of analysis geared to meet specific customer needs, they can win the same kind of customer appreciation and support as that enjoyed by government practitioners.

Statistical Tools

Additional decisionmaking tools derived from parametric or non-parametric statistical techniques, such as Bayesian analysis, are sometime used in intelligence. An exploration of them is beyond the scope of this study. Many of the statistically oriented tools continue to rely fundamentally on human judgment to assign values to variables, so that close attention to the types of reasoning and methods of analysis presented herein remain the fundamental analytical precondition to their use.[66]

---

[65] Clauser and Weir, 248-250.

[66] Editor's note: A former JMIC faculty member, Douglas E. Hunter, explores the intelligence applications of Bayesian Analysis in *Political/Military Applications of Bayesian Analysis: Methodological Issues* (Boulder, CO: Westview, 1984).

Analytic Mindset

Customer needs and collected information and data are not the only factors that influence the analytic process; the analyst brings his or her own unique thought patterns as well. This personal approach to problem-solving is "the distillation of the intelligence analyst's cumulative factual and conceptual knowledge into a framework for making estimative judgments on a complex subject."[67] Mindset helps intelligence analysts to put a situation into context, providing a frame of reference for examining the subject. Analysis could not take place if thinking were not bounded by such constructs. However, mindset can also lead analysts to apply certain viewpoints inappropriately or exclusively while neglecting other potentially enlightening perspectives on an issue. While no one can truly step outside his or her own mindset, becoming aware of potential analytic pitfalls can enable intelligence analysts to maximize the positive effects of mindset while minimizing the negatives.[68] Analysts can use the accompanying list of analytical pitfalls to determine which, if any, they may be applying in their work, and whether the relevant ones are accounted for in their analytic tasks.

Categories of Misperception and Bias[69]

Evoked-Set Reasoning: That information and concern which dominates one's thinking based on prior experience. One tends to uncritically relate new information to past or current dominant concerns.

Prematurely Formed Views: These spring from a desire for simplicity and stability, and lead to premature closure in the consideration of a problem.

Presumption that Support for One Hypothesis Disconfirms Others: Evidence that is consistent with one's preexisting beliefs is allowed to disconfirm other views. Rapid closure in the consideration of an issue is a problem.

Inappropriate Analogies: Perception that an event is analogous to past events, based on inadequate consideration of concepts or facts, or irrelevant criteria. Bias of "Representativeness."

Superficial Lessons From History: Uncritical analysis of concepts or events, superficial causality, over-generalization of obvious factors, inappropriate extrapolation from past success or failure.

Presumption of Unitary Action by Organizations: Perception that behavior of others is more planned, centralized, and coordinated than it really is. Dismisses accident and chaos. Ignores misperceptions of others. Fundamental attribution error, possibly caused by cultural bias.

---

[67] Jack Davis, "Combatting Mindset," *Studies in Intelligence* 35, no. 4 (Winter 1991): 13-18.

[68] Davis, "Combatting Mindset," 13-15.

[69] Excerpted from Dearth, "The Politics of Intelligence," 106-107.

Organizational Parochialism: Selective focus or rigid adherence to prior judgments based on organizational norms or loyalties. Can result from functional specialization. Group-think or stereotypical thinking.

Excessive Secrecy (Compartmentation): Over-narrow reliance on selected evidence. Based on concern for operational security. Narrows consideration of alternative views. Can result from or cause organizational parochialism.

Ethnocentrism: Projection of one's own culture, ideological beliefs, doctrine, or expectations on others. Exaggeration of the causal significance of one's own action. Can lead to mirror-imaging and wishful thinking. Parochialism.

Lack of Empathy: Undeveloped capacity to understand others' perception of their world, their conception of their role in that world, and their definition of their interests. Difference in cognitive contexts.

Mirror-Imaging: Perceiving others as one perceives oneself. Basis is ethnocentrism. Facilitated by closed systems and parochialism.

Ignorance: Lack of knowledge. Can result from prior-limited priorities or lack of curiosity, perhaps based on ethnocentrism, parochialism, denial of reality, rational-actor hypothesis (see next entry).

Rational-Actor Hypothesis: Assumption that others will act in a "rational" manner, based on one's own rational reference. Results from ethnocentrism, mirror-imaging, or ignorance.

Denial of Rationality: Attribution of irrationality to others who are perceived to act outside the bounds of one's own standards of behavior or decisionmaking. Opposite of rational-actor hypothesis. Can result from ignorance, mirror-imaging, parochialism, or ethnocentrism.

Proportionality Bias: Expectation that the adversary will expend efforts proportionate to the ends he seeks. Inference about the intentions of others from costs and consequences of actions they initiate.

Willful Disregard of New Evidence: Rejection of information that conflicts with already-held beliefs. Results from prior policy commitments, and/or excessive pursuit of consistency.

Image and Self-Image: Perception of what has been, is, will be, or should be (image as subset of belief system). Both inward-directed (self-image) and outward-directed (image). Both often influenced by self-absorption and ethnocentrism.

Defensive Avoidance: Refusal to perceive and understand extremely threatening stimuli. Need to avoid painful choices. Leads to wishful thinking.

Overconfidence in Subjective Estimates: Optimistic bias in assessment. Can result from premature or rapid closure of consideration, or ignorance.

Wishful Thinking (Pollyanna Complex): Hyper-credulity. Excessive optimism born of smugness and overconfidence.

Best-Case Analysis: Optimistic assessment based on cognitive predisposition and general beliefs of how others are likely to behave, or in support of personal or organizational interests or policy preferences.

Conservatism in Probability Estimation: In a desire to avoid risk, tendency to avoid estimating extremely high or extremely low probabilities. Routine thinking. Inclination to judge new phenomena in light of past experience, to miss essentially novel situational elements, or failure to reexamine established tenets. Tendency to seek confirmation of prior-held beliefs.

Worst-Case Analysis (Cassandra Complex): Excessive skepticism. Reflects pessimism and extreme caution, based on predilection (cognitive predisposition), adverse past experience, or on support of personal or organizational interests or policy preferences.

Because the biases and misperceptions outlined above can influence analysis, they may also affect the resultant analytic products. As explained in the following Part, analysis does not cease when intelligence production begins; indeed, the two are interdependent. The foregoing overview of analytic pitfalls should caution intelligence managers and analysts that intelligence products should remain as free as possible from such errors of omission and commission, yet still be tailored to the specific needs of customers. Consistently reminding intelligence producers of the dangers and benefits of mindset may help them avoid errors and polish their analytic skills. In addition, managers may conduct post-production evaluation of intelligence products, using the biases and misperceptions listed above to identify strengths and weaknesses in individual analysts' work, and to counsel them accordingly.

PART VI
PRODUCTION

Creating Intelligence

The previously-described steps of the intelligence process are necessary precursors to production, but it is only in this final step that functionality of the whole process is achieved. *Production* results in the creation of intelligence, that is, value-added actionable information tailored to a specific customer. In practical terms, production refers to the creation, in any medium, of either interim or *finished* briefings or reports for other analysts, or for decisionmakers or policy officials. As with elements of analysis developed in Part V, production principles described and explained here may apply to both government and private sector intelligence operations.

In government parlance, the term "finished" intelligence is reserved for products issued by analysts responsible for synthesizing all available sources of intelligence, resulting in a comprehensive assessment of an issue or situation, for use by senior analysts or decisionmakers. Creating finished intelligence for national and military customers is the role of CIA and DIA analysts, respectively. Analysts within an intelligence sub-discipline may also speak of a "finished" product from their point of view, meaning that intelligence from a single source, such as SIGINT, was interpreted as fully as possible in light of all other available intelligence from that source, plus any relevant published intelligence from other sources, and open source information. Analysts within the single-source intelligence agencies consider any information or intelligence not issued by their own organization to be "collateral."

Similar designations for finished intelligence products may apply in the business world. Particularly in large corporations with multidisciplinary intelligence units, or in business intelligence consulting firms, some production personnel may specialize in the creation of intelligence from a single source, while others specialize in finished reporting. For example, there may be specialists in library and on-line research, "HUMINT" experts who conduct interviews and attend conferences and trade shows, or scientists who perform experiments on products or materials. The reports generated by such personnel may be considered finished intelligence by their intended customers within subdivisions of the larger company. The marketing, product development, or public relations department of a corporation may consume single-source intelligence products designed to meet their individual needs. Such a large corporation may also have an intelligence synthesis unit that merges the reports from the specialized units into finished intelligence for use in strategic planning by senior decisionmakers. Similarly, in the intelligence consulting firm, each of the specialized production units may contribute their reports to a centralized finished intelligence unit which generates a synthesized product for the client.

Emphasizing the Customer's Bottom Line

The intelligence report or presentation must focus on the *results* of the analysis and make evident their significance through sound arguments geared to the customer's interests. In short, intelligence producers must BLUF their way through the presentation — that is, they must keep the "Bottom Line Up Front." This axiom applies not only to written expression, but also to oral briefings, or any other medium of expression used in the intelligence environment of government or business.

> It is often difficult for... intelligence [producers] to avoid the temptation to succumb to the Agatha Christie Syndrome. Like the great mystery writer, we want to keep our readers in suspense until we can deliver that "punch line." After we have worked hard on this analysis... we want the reader to know all the wonderful facts and analytical methods that have gone into our conclusions.... Most readers really will not care about all those bells and whistles that went into the analysis. *They want the bottom line*, and that is what intelligence professionals are paid to deliver.[70]

Knowing the customer enables the producer to generate intelligence that highlights the bottom line. Some customers are "big picture" thinkers, seeking a general overview of the issue, and guidance on the implications for their own position and responsibilities. An appropriate intelligence product for such a customer will be clear, concise, conclusive, and free of jargon or distracting detail.[71] Conversely, some customers are detail-oriented, seeing themselves as the ultimate expert on the subject area. This type of customer needs highly detailed and specialized intelligence to supplement and amplify known information. The broad-brush approach to intelligence will not only miss the mark with this customer, but may actually be perceived as an insult, lessening the chances that future products by the offending producer will be accepted or used.[72] Producers should therefore tailor both the content and delivery of the intelligence to the customer. The following section provides guidelines for creating intelligence products that meet customer needs.[73]

Anatomy of an Intelligence Product

Whether it is produced within the government, or in the business setting, the basic nature of the intelligence product remains the same. The analyst creates a product to document ongoing research, give the customer an update on a current issue or situation, or

---

[70] James S. Major, *The Style Guide: Research and Writing at the Joint Military Intelligence College*, (Washington DC: Joint Military Intelligence College, August 1994): 345.

[71] Mathams, 88.

[72] Davis, *Analytic Tradecraft*, 7.

[73] The Central Intelligence Agency has published an unclassified collection of essays on techniques for producing finished national security intelligence. The purpose of the collection is to document best practices, and to reach out to academia and the public. Its title emphasizes the instrumentality of analysis to production. See Central Intelligence Agency, *A Compendium of Analytic Tradecraft Notes*, (Washington, DC, Directorate of Intelligence· February 1997)

provide an estimate of expected target activity. In general terms, the product's function is to cover one or more subject areas, or to be used by the customer for a particular application. Along with these aspects, additional dimensions of the intelligence product are summarized in the table below. They are more fully described in the following paragraphs.

Table 11: Dimensions of an Intelligence Product

Source: Author

Dimension Category	Dimension	Examples
Content	Subject	Biographical, economic, geographic, military, political, science and technology, sociology, transportation and communications
	Intended Use	Research, current, estimative, operational, science and technology, warning
Features	Timeliness	Short-/long-term, opportune, routine/priority
	Periodicity	Ad hoc/scheduled; analyst/customer-initiated
	Scope	Narrow/broad; detailed/summary; basic/exhaustive
Packaging	Medium	Hard/softcopy, written/oral, video
	Format	Formal/informal, textual/graphical
Customer	Relationship to producer	Intended/incidental recipient; internal/external; novice/expert
	Distribution method	Internal/external; direct/indirect; focused/broad

Content

Determination of product content is done in close cooperation with the customer, sometimes at the initiative of one or the other, often in a cycle of give-and-take of ideas. Formal intelligence requirements, agreed upon by both producer and customer in advance, do drive the production process, but the converse is also true. The intelligence unit's own self-concept and procedures influence its choice of which topics to cover, and which aspects to emphasize. As a result, the customer comes to expect a certain type of product from that unit, and adjusts requirement statements accordingly. In addition, the intelligence process may bring to light aspects of the target that neither the producer nor customer anticipated. When the parties involved have a close working relationship, either one may receive inspiration from interim products, and take the lead in pursuing new ways to exploit the target.[74]

Often, this dialogue centers around the pursuit of new sources associated with known lucrative sources. Examples from government include HUMINT targeting of persons identified in SIGINT as having access to foreign leaders, and SIGINT targeting of communications equipment revealed in IMINT of a foreign military installation. Parallel business examples might include intelligence personnel following leads to new sources revealed in original research or a published report: A pharmaceutical industry analyst who reads a business intelligence report about current breast cancer treatments may then investigate how to access human and documentary sources mentioned in the report, for further information on new drug therapy options for the disease.

The basic orientation of the intelligence product toward a particular subject or application is also determined by the producer-customer relationship. Frequently, the intelligence service will organize the production process and its output to mirror the customer organization. Government production by the single-source intelligence agencies is largely organized geographically or topically, to meet the needs of all-source country, region, or topic analysts in the finished-intelligence producing agencies, such as DIA or the National Counterintelligence Center. In the private sector, some intelligence consultant firms are specializing in one subject area, and gearing all production to one customer set, such as the petroleum industry.

In terms of intended use by the customer, both business and government producers may generate intelligence to be applied in the current, estimative, operational, research, science and technology, or warning context. Serendipity plays a role here, because the collected and analyzed information may meet any or all of these criteria. A good example is warning intelligence. Military and political analysts are always alert for target indications that an emergency, such as outbreak of war, or a political coup, is imminent. Standing procedures dictate that routine operations switch to warning mode in this case, so that time-sensitive intelligence on the situation can be issued to all relevant customers. Business intelligence analysts may also find themselves in the warning role unexpectedly, when they make discoveries that have significant time-sensitive implications for customer decisions and actions.

Features

Three key features of the intelligence product are timeliness, scope, and periodicity. Timeliness includes not only the amount of time required to deliver the product, but also the usefulness of the product to the customer at a given moment. Scope involves the level of detail or comprehensiveness of the material contained in the product. Periodicity describes the schedule of product initiation and generation.

---

[74] Turner, 314-320.

In intelligence production, the adage "timing is everything" is particularly apt. When a customer requests specific support, and when actionable information is discovered through collection and analysis, the resultant intelligence product is irrelevant unless the customer receives it in time to take action — by adapting to or influencing the target entity. Timeliness therefore encompasses the short-term or long-term duration of the production process, and the degree to which the intelligence itself proves opportune for the customer. In addition, the relative priority of the intelligence contained in the product affects the timeliness calculus. For example, a business intelligence analyst conducting research for a consumer electronics corporation may produce short-term routine reports as new information becomes available. A long-term routine summary report may be the final output from this project. However, a short-term priority report may result at any time, if time-sensitive information on competitor capabilities or intentions comes to light.

The scope of an intelligence product describes both the amount of material it contains and the depth of coverage it provides on the topic. Its focus may be narrow or broad, and the content may be detailed or in summary form. The level of coverage may be basic or exhaustive. All of these aspects are determined by the customer's needs, and by the amount and extent of the source material available.

> The amount of detail distributed will depend on the circumstances and the requirements of the user. Time constraints often will determine how much detail is given. There may be such a wealth of detail on a particular subject that an analyst might spend a month or more making a detailed analysis, but the urgency of the need for the intelligence may be such as to make a brief survey, produced in two days, much more valuable. It is important to remember that many users of intelligence have neither the time nor the patience to read through a voluminous study, however excellent it may be, and would much prefer to have the essential elements of the analysis set down in a few succinct paragraphs. Some users, however, do require detail, and when that is the case it should be provided in a usable form.[75]

Periodicity is also linked to validated customer requirements. Intelligence products correspond to requirements that specify responsiveness criteria, thus production may occur on an *ad hoc* basis or on a schedule. Analysts may proactively generate products to meet known needs of specific customers, or they may respond to spontaneous customer requests for tailored intelligence. Furthermore, "analysts, as experts in their fields, are expected to initiate studies that address questions yet unformulated by [customers]."[76] By selecting from available source material, and determining when to issue an intelligence product, analysts have the potential to influence how their customers use intelligence to make policy decisions.[77] In the government, topic experts may become close advisors to National Intelligence Officers or directly to senior policymakers. In

---

[75] Mathams, 92.

[76] Turner, 319.

[77] Turner, 320.

the business world, a sharp intelligence analyst might be responsible for a dramatic change in a retail company's focus, by identifying emerging consumer trends and sensitizing management for the need to reorient the company. To effect this change, the company would become dependent on intelligence about competitors in the same industry. For example, an analyst's assessment of consumer interest in buying natural pet foods might stimulate requirements for further studies, and might lead a manufacturer to change its products to meet consumer demand, before another company captures that market.

Packaging

Government intelligence products are typically packaged as highly structured written and oral presentations, including electrical messages, hardcopy reports, and briefings.[78] Many organizations also generate video intelligence products, especially in the form of live daily "newscasts," or canned documentary presentations. However, the production landscape is being transformed by technology, and today, a wide range of options is available to both business and government. Modern telecommunications and software make possible a whole new world of intelligence production, in which all the players, including customers, are in constant interaction. The Department of Defense, for example, has devised the Joint Intelligence Virtual Architecture (JIVA) concept to accelerate and streamline the entire intelligence process. Under JIVA, intelligence personnel will use advanced communication and analysis tools to electronically collaborate with each other and their customers, resulting in improved timeliness and customization of Defense intelligence products.[79] Part of the JIVA concept is the use of on-line product modules that can stand alone as finished intelligence, or be synergistically combined with other modules for use by interim or ultimate customers.[80] Similar collaborative production techniques may be successful in large business intelligence units with geographically dispersed personnel and customers. However, the benefits offered by modern intelligence practices such as JIVA also present significant challenges, including the financial and political investment in new infrastructure, and the legal implications of the required cooperation between the government and technology firms.[81]

The format of the intelligence product, regardless of the medium used to convey it, affects how well it is received by the customer. Even in a multimedia presentation, the personal touch can make a positive difference. Therefore, the degree of formality, and the mix of textual and graphical material should match the customer's preferences. Some cus-

---

[78] A guide to orally presenting intelligence is found in James S. Major, *Briefing with Intelligence*, (Washington DC: Joint Military Intelligence College, August 1997).

[79] Defense Intelligence Agency, *Vector 21, A Strategic Plan for the Defense Intelligence Agency* (Washington, DC: Programs and Operations Staff, undated), 20.

[80] Louis E. Andre, "Intelligence Production: Towards a Knowledge-Based Future," *Defense Intelligence Journal* 6, no. 2 (Fall 1997): 41.

[81] William O. Studeman, "Leading Intelligence Along the Byways of Our Future: Acquiring C4ISR Architectures for the 21st Century," *Defense Intelligence Journal* 7, no. 1 (Spring 1998): 52.

tomers want formal briefings, while others enjoy conversational give and take; some want a scheduled meeting, others want the analyst to be available at any time for impromptu consultation. Often, verbally oriented customers request one-on-one exchanges during official travel in automobiles or in airplanes. Conversely, the visually oriented customer may prefer video clips, graphs, charts, and photographs, accompanied by brief amplifying text. Many customers prefer written analyses, often in the form of concise executive summaries or point papers; some will ask for an in-depth study after consuming the initial or periodic assessment. However, producers should be aware of the potential pitfalls of relying on the executive summary to reach key customers. If the product does not appeal to the executive's staff members who read it first, it may never reach the intended recipient.[82]

Customer

In addition to understanding the customer's intelligence requirements, the producer may benefit from an awareness of the relationship between the customer organization and the intelligence service itself. Status issues between the two parties may influence the tone of the intelligence product. Aspects of the producer-customer relationship include whether the recipient is the intended or incidental customer, whether the customer is internal or external to the intelligence service, and whether the parties differ in their level of subject matter knowledge.

The intelligence producer selects the product content and format to suit a specific individual or customer set. However, the producer should beware of selecting material or phraseology that is too esoteric or personal for a potential wide audience. Intelligence products are official publications that become official records for use by all authorized personnel within the producer and customer organizations. They should focus on the primary customer's needs, yet address the interests of other legitimate players. Sometimes, when the producer is struggling with how to meet the needs of both internal and external customers, the solution is to create two different types of products, one for each type of customer. Internal products contain details about the sources and methods used to generate the intelligence, while external products emphasize actionable target information. Similarly, the producer adjusts the product content and tone to the customer's level of expertise. For example, a SIGINT producer may issue a highly technical and detailed product for fellow SIGINT service members, but for intelligence producers in a different agency, a less technical but still producer-oriented product may be appropriate. Similarly, the business intelligence producer within a marketing department may generate a highly specialized report for the head of the department, but may issue an executive summary for the company president.

Selection of the distribution method for the product is also closely tied to the relationship between producer and customer. The ability to deliver specific types of products to internal and external customers depends upon available infrastructure and

---

[82] Loch K. Johnson, *America's Secret Power, The CIA in a Democratic Society,* (New York: Oxford University Press, 1989): 98

resources (telecommunications lines, transportation, media equipment). Politics affect whether intelligence can be delivered by the individual analyst directly to the customer, or only through a chain of command. Finally, the number of designated recipients is often determined by the sensitivity of the intelligence issue covered in the product. If the intelligence is highly sensitive, such as a report on threats to the president's life, then only the few involved persons (the president and a few key security personnel) will receive the report. A routine report may be broadly distributed to a large customer set. Thus, the choice of distribution method is more a marketing decision than a mechanical exercise.[83] Successful delivery of a truly useful intelligence product to a receptive customer is the result of communication and cooperation among all the players.

Customer Feedback and Production Evaluation

The production phase of the intelligence process does not end with delivering the product to the customer. Rather, it continues in the same manner in which it began: with dialogue between producer and customer.

> If the product is really to be useful for policy-making and command, dissemination involves feedback, which is part of the marketing function.... Ideally, the "marketer" who delivers the product is the same individual who accepts and helps to refine the initial requirement.[84]

Intelligence producers need feedback from end-users. If producers do not learn what is useful and not useful to customers, they cannot create genuine intelligence. Internal review procedures that focus on the format and style of intelligence products are not sufficient for producers to judge their performance; they must hear from customers on the intelligence value of their work. Then producers can modify their practices to further develop those activities that served the customer well, and improve or eliminate those that did not.

Feedback procedures between producers and customers should include key questions, such as: Is the product usable? Is it timely? Was it in fact used? Did the product meet expectations? If not, why not? What next? The answers to these questions will lead to refined production, greater use of intelligence by decisionmakers, and further feedback sessions. Thus, production of intelligence actually generates more requirements in this iterative process.[85] Producers and managers may use the framework developed by Brei and summarized below as an initial checklist for evaluating their own work, and as a basis for formal customer surveys to obtain constructive feedback.

Producers also need performance feedback from their own managers. Useful aspects of such an internal evaluation may include whether the output met the conditions set down by customers and producers in formal intelligence requirements, whether the intel-

---

[83] Johnson, 97.
[84] Dearth, "National Intelligence," 20.
[85] Dearth, "National Intelligence," 20.

ligence was indeed used by customers, and whether the product resulted from a high standard of analytic quality.[86] To establish a formal internal review process for monitoring the quality of analysis in intelligence products, managers could select experienced analysts to serve on a rotating basis as "mindset coaches" — reviewing assessments for issues of mindset, uncertainty, and policy utility, or consider pairing with another production division to swap personnel for this activity. As a rule, the less the critical reader knows about the substance of the paper the more he or she will concentrate on the quality of the argumentation. A reward for the best "mindset coaches" would be to make them branch chiefs.[87]

Table 12: A Framework for Intelligence Product Evaluation and Customer Feedback
Source: adapted from Brei

Accuracy: Were all sources and data free of technical error, misperception, and hostile efforts to mislead?

Objectivity: Were all judgments free of deliberate distortions and manipulations due to self-interest?

Usability: Was all production issued in a form that facilitated ready comprehension and immediate application? Were products compatible with the customer's capabilities for receiving, manipulating, protecting, and storing the product?

Relevance: Was information selected and organized for its applicability to a customer's requirements, with potential consequences and significance of the information made explicit to the customer's circumstances?

Readiness: Are intelligence systems responsive to the existing and contingent intelligence requirements of customers at all levels of command?

Timeliness: Was intelligence delivered while the content was still actionable under the customer's circumstances?

Management's role extends beyond fostering quality production, to bearing responsibility for organizing and administering the complete intelligence process. Managers make key decisions that mirror the intelligence process and make production possible. In conjunction with customers, managers determine what customer set the intelligence unit will serve; what sources it will exploit; what types of intelligence it will produce; and what methods of collection, processing, analysis, production, customer feedback, and self-evaluation it will use. The following Part of this primer explores best practices in managing the intelligence process.

---

[86] Arthur S. Hulnick, "Managing Intelligence Analysis," 338.
[87] Davis, "Mindset," 17.

PART VII
MANAGING THE INTELLIGENCE PROCESS

The Role of Management

Another discipline integral to the intelligence profession — but worthy of special consideration in this context — is that of management. The effective administration and direction of intelligence activities can be regarded as the epitome of intelligence professionalism. Just as an untutored civilian cannot be expected competently to command [a military unit], so an untrained or inexperienced layperson cannot be expected effectively to direct [an intelligence operation]. But mastery of professional intelligence skills does not, in itself, ensure that a person is able to direct intelligence functions competently; expertise in administrative techniques and behavioral skills is also essential to managerial effectiveness. Some facility in these areas can be acquired through experience, but a professional level of competence requires familiarity with the principles and theories of management, and leadership.[88]

Moreover, supervisors and managers have a particular responsibility for ensuring the professional development of their subordinates. When all the members of the intelligence unit are competent, then the effectiveness of the group increases. Enabling subordinates also frees managers to thoroughly plan and administer the intelligence operation, instead of redoing the work of production personnel. Meanwhile, managers may continue to broaden their own knowledge of the intelligence process and its customer-service mission.[89]

Organizing the Intelligence Service

In the national Intelligence Community, federal laws form the basis for a centrally coordinated but functionally organized system. The Director of Central Intelligence (DCI) leads the community with the aid of the National Intelligence Council (NIC). Members of the NIC come from all the intelligence agencies plus academia and the private sector. The

---

[88] George Allen, "The Professionalization of Intelligence," in Dearth and Goodden, 1995, 37. Informed debate on the realities of analysts' and managers' intelligence responsibilities toward customers is ongoing in the *International Journal of Intelligence and CounterIntelligence*. Examples of this literature are: Michael A. Turner, "Setting Analytical Priorities in U.S. Intelligence," 9, no. 3 (Fall 1996): 313-327; H. Bradford Westerfield, "Inside Ivory Bunkers: CIA Analysts Resist Managers' "Pandering" Part I, 9, no. 4 (Winter 1996/97): 407-424; and H. Bradford Westerfield, "Inside Ivory Bunkers: CIA Analysts Resist Managers' "Pandering" Part II, 10, no. 1 (Spring 1997): 19-54.

[89] Russell G. Swenson, *An Office Manager's Guide to Intelligence Readiness*, Occasional Paper Number Three (Washington, DC: JMIC, December 1996), 3-5.

NIC manages the national Intelligence Needs Process and supervises the production of National Intelligence Estimates for senior policymakers. Other senior bodies advise or assist the DCI in matters of policy, resource management, performance review, coordination of elements, customer relations, and intra-community relations.[90] Four topical intelligence centers staffed by multiple agencies coordinate intelligence production for policymakers in the key areas of Counterterrorism, Counterintelligence, Counternarcotics, and Nonproliferation.[91] Crisis situations may spark the formation of a temporary special task force, integrating intelligence functions that are usually separate. Although the national Intelligence Community is centrally coordinated, each member organization develops some self-determined policies and procedures, and engages in competitive analysis with respect to the other organizations.

The unifying principle across government intelligence missions is the basic charter to monitor and manage threats to national interests and to the intelligence service itself. In both the national Intelligence Community and the business community, managers may make a distinction between self-protective intelligence activities and competitive intelligence activities. Self-protection involves gathering and analyzing data about threats to public, personal, or multinational mission members' security, whereas competitive activities involve gathering and analyzing data about adversary organizations or countries. In business, the two functions are sometimes undertaken by entirely different companies or groups within the same company.[92] Government subordinates both functions within the intelligence infrastructure.

Table 13: Three Contexts for Government and Business Intelligence Tasks
Source: Author and Editor

Contexts:	Individual	Corporate	Global
Government Tasks:	Diplomatic Security/ Force Protection	Foreign Capabilities Assessment	Strategic Warning from Intelligence
Business Tasks:	Threat Analysis, Personal Risk Analysis	Business/Competitive Intelligence	Business Scenario Planning

Threat analysis in the business environment depends on the open exchange of information between companies, as it is widely recognized that no one benefits from other companies encountering unnecessary risk or danger to their personnel. On the other hand, at the corporate level, competitive business intelligence relies on the protection or discovery of important corporate data. In the public security environment, diplomatic security and

---

[90] CIA, *Consumer's Guide*, 2-3.

[91] Davis, *Opportunity Analysis*, 8.

[92] Jonathan Tetzlaff, Area Director, Security Research and Analysis, Amoco Corporation, personal correspondence with editor, 24 October 1997.

force protection for a government's own citizens, and for personnel in multilateral operations, is in the best interests of all. Conversely, foreign capabilities assessment operates in the context of a zero-sum game among countries, with potential winners and losers of the tactical advantage.

When the very survival of a corporation or country is at stake vis-a-vis other players in their respective environments, a global or strategic model applies. At this level, strategic warning intelligence takes center stage in the government security setting, and its counterpart — strategic scenario planning — achieves value in the private sector. Scenario planning has been used advantageously by some companies. The Shell Oil Company, for example, used scenario planning to justify disinvestment in oil exploitation infrastructure prior to the worldwide fall in oil demand in the 1980s. The company rose from 14th to 2nd place among oil multinationals, as overinvested companies lost billions.[93] The alternative to taking global or strategic intelligence action is to allow threats to emerge and to bring company or government officials to the realm of crisis management. There, fundamental government or business interests are at stake, and the outcome is more likely to be left to the vagaries of impulse and chance than to the considered judgment and actions of corporate or government leaders.

Private sector intelligence services can consider which elements of the national intelligence model may apply in their own domain. Will the organization require central coordination of diverse elements as the national system does, or might the intelligence unit more closely resemble a single collector or producer agency with a simpler management structure? Will an advisory group mediate between intelligence producers and customers, and does the intelligence service require its own staff to coordinate operations? Will the service be organized functionally into collection and production elements, or perhaps topically? Is

---

[93] Robbie E. Davis-Floyd, "Storytelling Corporate Futures: The Shell Scenarios," *International Journal of Futures Studies* 1 (1995-1997), on-line at http://www.systems.org/HTML/journals.htm, accessed 3 December 1997. The purpose of scenario planning is to force business managers and executives to face future uncertainties squarely by elaborating and evaluating the likelihood and impact of alternative hypothetical business environments. Dissenters are valued, rather than avoided, and, as in government intelligence channels, information is proactively developed to champion and refute the various scenarios as "controllable" pathways to the future. Recent reviews of business scenario planning include Kathy Moyer, "Scenario Planning at British Airways — A Case Study," *Long Range Planning* 29, No. 2 (April 1996): 172-181; Francoise Hecht, "The Aha! Factor," *Director* 50, No. 12 (July 1997): 59; and Ian Smith, "Avoiding Future Shock," *Director* 50, No. 12 (July 1997): 56-59.

A seminal work on the analytical environment for strategic warning in government intelligence is Ephraim Kam, *Surprise Attack* (Cambridge, MA: Harvard University Press, 1988). Although Kam focuses on military attack scenarios, the arena for strategic warning in government intelligence work has expanded as international security concerns shift toward economic competition and away from military confrontation. The convergence of economics and security signals a need for benchmarking the intelligence process, and could presage an era of greater collaboration between cells of intelligence analysts and policymakers at the highest levels, not unlike the give and take that characterizes successful business scenario planning.

the intelligence service an independent organization with external customers, or does it operate within a parent organization? If the latter, does each department, such as Marketing, Planning, or Research require its own tailored intelligence support? Does the chief executive require a centralized intelligence service, by whatever name, to assist in corporate policy-making? Should the service develop contingency plans for providing time-sensitive support in a crisis situation? On a larger scale, should intelligence services within an industry pool their resources for mutual benefit in a crisis environment, or to proactively adapt to a changing environment, as does the national Intelligence Community? The answers to these questions may help private sector intelligence organizations determine how closely to pattern their structure after that of the national intelligence system.

Managing Analysis and Production

Intelligence managers in government and industry need to decide how to organize the production process just as they need to determine the structure of the intelligence service as a whole. Typical methods of assigning analysts are by target function, geographical region, technical subject, or policy issue. The intelligence service may task analysts to concentrate on one type of source information, or to merge all available sources to produce "finished" intelligence or estimates. Some industries will need analysts to specialize in certain technical subject areas or complex issues, while large corporations may assign intelligence analysts to each of several departments such as Research or Product Development. Small independent intelligence services may require personnel to perform all the functions of the intelligence process from needs assessment to production and performance evaluation. In that case, analysts might be assigned to a particular customer account rather than a specific topic area. Part VIII of this primer presents findings on the attributes of intelligence analysts that may prove useful in determining how to allocate human resources in the intelligence production process.

> Some characterizations of the analytic mission...seem to emphasize serving the policymaking process as an abstraction: to tell it like it is, to level the playing field, to keep the policymakers honest, to be right on the record.... But excessive adherence to these attributes can cause overproduction of assessments that feature what analysts think policy officials should want to know, and underproduction of assessments featuring what officials think they need from...analytic specialists.... To provide the requisite benefits for policymakers, the analytic assessments of the intelligence production unit have to deliver a high order of understanding and insight that can support sound decisionmaking. One should avoid a definition of effective analysis that emphasizes accurate prediction...or one that centers on whether or not a policy worked.[94]

> Furthermore, managers can take the initiative in transforming intelligence into a proactive service. Managers who are isolated from the intelligence customer tend to monitor the quantity of reports produced and level of polish in intelligence products, but not the utility of the intelligence itself.[95]

---

[94] Davis, *Opportunity Analysis*, 2-3.
[95] Davis, *Opportunity Analysis*, 10.

But policy officials will seek information and judgment from the source that provides it at the lowest personal cost, including the mass media, no matter how much money the intelligence organization is spending to fund analysis on their behalf. Thus, managers need to learn to ask for and accept opportunity analysis included in intelligence products, not remove it as inappropriate during the review process. One way to ensure that analysts produce truly useful intelligence is for managers to take an inventory, say twice per year, of the specific professional interests of their key [customers]. Policy officials are more comfortable thinking in terms of outputs than of inputs. Thus, the inventory should be couched in terms of the policymakers' objectives — their hopes and fears — and not in terms of their "intelligence priorities."... The intelligence manager should then take responsibility for converting the inventory into signals for the restructuring of collection, research, and analytic production.[96]

Evaluating the Intelligence Process

Beyond organizing and monitoring intelligence production, an additional management responsibility is to evaluate the intelligence service's overall mission performance. From the manager's perspective, intelligence products are not the only output from the intelligence process; therefore, products are not the only focus of rigorous self-evaluation. In the course of its operations, the intelligence unit expends and generates significant amounts of financial and political capital. Careful examination of this commodity flow may yield key insights into process improvement. Internal review procedures may thus include measures of how well the intelligence service and its components organize their work, use funds, allocate materiel and human resources, and coordinate with parent and customer organizations, all from the self-interested perspective of the intelligence service itself. To assist them in this effort, managers may evaluate the sub-processes and interim products of the Needs Definition, Collection, Processing, Analysis, and Production phases of the intelligence process in terms of Brei's Intelligence Values: Accuracy, Objectivity, Usability, Relevance, Readiness, and Timeliness.

Furthermore, to put a human face on intelligence process, conscientious managers may wish to include in their internal review a frank analysis of their own personnel management record. Perhaps a new definition of "customer" is in order for carrying out this aspect of intelligence evaluation. Seeing the members of the intelligence service as customers of management, and of each other, can enable managers to create a work culture in which each person's needs and talents are respected and incorporated into the organization's mission. By subscribing to the philosophy that a happy workforce is a productive workforce, managers may also achieve the organizational goal of satisfying external customer requirements. With this purpose in mind, principles for matching intelligence personnel to appropriate job assignments are discussed in the next Part of this primer.

---

[96] Davis, *Opportunity Analysis*, 6.

PART VIII
PORTRAIT OF AN INTELLIGENCE
ANALYST

The efficacy of the intelligence process described in the foregoing chapters depends upon personnel who are both able and willing to do the specialized work required. Through the findings of several government studies, this section presents the ideal characteristics of the central figure in value-added production — the intelligence analyst. According to these studies, the successful intelligence analyst brings to the discipline certain requisite knowledges and abilities, or has a high aptitude for acquiring them through specialized training; is able to perform the specific tasks associated with the job; and exhibits personality traits compatible with intelligence analysis work. This profile will remain valid in any setting modeled after the national security intelligence system.

The cognitive, performance and personality attributes of the intelligence analyst are explained below. Readers are encouraged to apply this information in accordance with their own particular circumstances. For example:

> Incumbents and individuals considering employment in intelligence analysis may deepen their self-awareness and assess their potential for success and satisfaction in this profession.

> Educators and recruiters may identify and prepare candidates for employment in intelligence analysis.

> Managers and supervisors may make enlightened decisions about selection, placement, tasking and evaluation of intelligence analysis personnel.

Cognitive Attributes

An individual's analytic skill results from a combination of innate qualities, acquired experience, and relevant education. Psychologists call these mental faculties cognitive attributes, and further divide them into two types: abilities (behavioral traits, being able to perform a task) and knowledges (learned information about a specific subject).[97] Whereas an individual's cognitive abilities are relatively fixed by the time he or she enters the job market, knowledges are situation-specific and can be acquired through training.[98]

According to a recent formal job analysis of selected intelligence analysts conducted by the NSA Office of Human Resources Services, important cognitive abilities for intelligence analysis include written expression, reading comprehension, inductive reasoning, deductive reasoning, pattern recognition, oral comprehension, and information

---

[97] Mark H. Haucke, Industrial Psychologist, NSA, interview with the author, 25 May 1995.
[98] Melissie C. Rumizen, Benchmarking Manager, NSA, interview with the author, 5 July 1996.

59

ordering.[99] Furthermore, both junior analysts and experienced analysts or supervisors agree that high levels of these abilities are necessary for performing the intelligence analysis job. The abilities are defined in the box below.

Cognitive Abilities Required of Intelligence Analysts[100]

Written Expression: The ability to use words and sentences in writing so others will understand. Involves knowledge of the meanings and distinctions among words, knowledge of grammar, and the ability to organize sentences and paragraphs.

Reading Comprehension: The ability to read and understand written sentences and paragraphs.

Inductive Reasoning: The ability to combine separate pieces of information, or specific answers to problems, to form general rules or conclusions. Involves the ability to think of possible reasons why things go together. Also includes coming up with a logical explanation for a series of events that seem unrelated.

Deductive Reasoning: The ability to apply general rules to specific problems to come up with a logical resolution. Involves deciding if the resolution makes sense.

Pattern Recognition: The ability to identify or detect a known pattern (a figure, word, or object) that is hidden in other material.

Oral Comprehension: The ability to listen and understand spoken words and sentences.

Information Ordering: The ability to follow a rule or set of rules in order to arrange things or actions in a meaningful order. The rule or set of rules to be used must already be given. The things or actions to be put in order can include numbers, letters, words, pictures, procedures, sentences, and mathematical or logical operations.

One set of junior analysts and another of supervisors were separately asked to judge the importance of each of these abilities in performing the intelligence analysis job (see Table 14). Junior analysts assign greater importance to two abilities (written expression and inductive reasoning), but significantly less importance to pattern recognition, than do their supervisors. These results have implications for staffing the intelligence analysis job in both the government and private sector. For example, if junior analysts place greater importance on written expression than their supervisors do, they may be frustrated to receive less training, tasking and recognition than needed for this aspect of their job. The discrepancies in the rankings among the five abilities judged most important by the two groups can be addressed individually by managers. However, the rankings provide some useful generalizations for identifying cognitive attributes applicable to any intelligence environment. In the case of the National Security Agency, the results presented here led

---

[99] Data were generated by Mark H. Haucke, Industrial Psychologist, using a Management Research Institute (MRI) survey instrument presented in *Ability and Knowledge Requirements* (Bethesda, MD: MRI, 1994).

[100] Adapted from MRI, *Ability and Knowledge Requirements.*

psychologists to design a job-relevant pre-employment aptitude exam for intelligence analysts.

Table 14: Comparative Ranking of Cognitive Abilities Thought to Be Required for Intelligence Analysis
(The lower the number on the 1 to 5 scale, the higher the perceived importance of the ability)
Source: Author and Haucke Study

Cognitive Ability	GROUP 1 (23 Junior Analysts - less than 7 years experience)	GROUP 2 (18 Supervisors — older generation; Ave. Years experience: 19)
Written Expression	1	3
Reading Comprehension	2	1
Inductive Reasoning	2	3
Deductive Reasoning	3	2
Pattern Recognition	3	1
Oral Comprehension	4	4
Information Ordering	5	4

Unlike the abilities categories, areas of knowledge for government intelligence specialists do not necessarily apply to their private sector counterparts. The formal job study of government intelligence analysts revealed that knowledge of military-related and technical subjects, not surprisingly, was prevalent among the individuals in the research group.[101] However, in either public or private sectors, managers can hire and train personnel to apply the requisite knowledges in a given job. A next logical step is to define the components of the intelligence analysis job, to be able to plan and assess individual job performance.

Performance Factors

Even as the analysis described above examined cognitive inputs to the job, a related performance review project, also at NSA, described intelligence analysts' output on the job. As part of this review, supervisors of intelligence analysts placed their subordinates' mission-essential job tasks into seven categories. Next, they evaluated the job performance of

---

[101] Data courtesy of Dr. Mark Haucke.

intelligence analysts according to those criteria. Researchers found a strong positive correlation between aptitude for intelligence analysis (as measured in the knowledges and abilities survey) and successful job performance (as rated by supervisors).[102] Following is a brief description of the seven intelligence analysis performance categories:[103]

Data Collection - Research and gather data from all available sources.

Data Monitoring - Review flow of scheduled incoming data.

Data Organizing - Organize, format, and maintain data for analysis and technical report generation.

Data Analysis - Analyze gathered data to identify patterns, relationships, or anomalies.

Data Interpretation/Communication - Assign meaning to analyzed data and communicate it to appropriate parties.

Computer Utilization - Use computer applications to assist in analysis.

Coordination - Coordinate with internal and external organizations.

This concise inventory echoes the intelligence process and illustrates the complexity of the intelligence analyst's job. It also serves as a blueprint for managers as they design intelligence organizations and individual personnel assignments. In particular, the analyst's job description should reflect these expected behaviors for purposes of recruitment, selection, placement, training, and performance evaluation. The intelligence organization should also be structured physically and logically to enable these functions to occur. Managers should consider how all these factors combine to determine the effectiveness of individual analysts, intelligence units, and even national agencies or private firms that produce and use intelligence.

Personality Traits

The third component of the intelligence analyst profile, personality traits, addresses the individual's preferences for behaving in certain ways under specific conditions. Adults tend to exhibit the same set of behavior preferences consistently in familiar situations. This behavior pattern may be identified as a personality type. One well-known instrument for identifying an individual's personality type is the Myers-Briggs Type Indicator (MBTI).[104] The following discussion of the intelligence analyst's personality is based upon MBTI research.

---

[102] Haucke interview, 13 June 1996.

[103] Standardized categories are presented in an MRI performance evaluation booklet, *Job Dimension Ratings* (Bethesda, MD: MRI, 1995).

[104] See Isabel Briggs Myers, *Introduction to Type.* (Palo Alto, CA: Consulting Psychologists Press, 1980), and Ronald D. Garst, *Intelligence Types: The Role of Personality in the Intelligence Profession.* 2d printing, (Washington, DC: Joint Military Intelligence College, August 1995).

Personality types are associated with more or less predictable patterns of behavior — meaning that people of different personality types approach tasks differently and have different tastes, interests, likes and dislikes. For example, some people would rather work alone while others prefer to work with other people. Some enjoy working with concrete information, others with abstract information. Some decide on the basis of personal reasons, some on cold, hard logic. And finally, some people enjoy making decisions while others are reluctant to decide because of perceived information inadequacy.[105]

Research at the Joint Military Intelligence College (JMIC) demonstrates that intelligence professionals exhibit a pattern of personality traits that sets them apart from the U.S. population as a whole. In this regard, intelligence professionals are no different from many others, for every profession has its own distinct pattern of personality traits. A significant percentage (21 percent) of those who choose to pursue employment in national security intelligence tend to express the following behavior preferences: orientation to the inner world of ideas rather than the outer world of things and people, tendency to gather factual information through the senses rather than inspiration, proclivity to make decisions on the basis of logic rather than emotion, and an eagerness to seek closure proactively instead of leaving possibilities open. In contrast, researchers found that people who exhibit the opposite set of personality traits are almost non-existent among intelligence professionals. The chart below summarizes the terminology by which the MBTI describes personality traits. Note that the most frequently occurring type among the respondents to the JMIC survey exhibit the traits I, S, T and J.[106]

The JMIC data are based on a large sample of government intelligence students and practitioners. Persons engaged in the study or practice of other forms of intelligence, particularly in the private sector, should not expect their personality type to match the JMIC profile. However, intelligence practitioners who choose and successfully apply the intelligence methodology presented in this primer are likely to exhibit the same personality traits as those identified in government practitioners. Because people tend to be satisfied and productive in their work if their own personalities match the corresponding behaviors suitable to their jobs, this research tying personality traits to the intelligence profession can help individuals consider their general suitability for certain types of intelligence work.

---

[105] Garst, *Intelligence Types*, 1.
[106] Garst, *Intelligence Types*, 9.

Personality Aspects Measured by the MBTI[107]

Orientation to the world

E=Extraversion

Orientation to the outer world of things and people, interacting with and affecting them

I=Introversion

Orientation to the inner world of ideas and concepts, solitude and self-awareness

Perception: non-rational processes; awareness of things, people, events or ideas, selection of stimuli to attend to

S=Sensing

Gather information by physical sensation; oriented to facts, detail and the present

N=Intuitive

Gather information by inspiration, unconscious processes; oriented to possibilities, relationships, and the future

Judgment: ways of deciding, evaluating, choosing, selecting

T=Thinking

Decide on basis of logic, impersonal objective criteria, cause and effect, laws and justice

F=Feeling

Decide on basis of subjective, personal criteria and values, and how decisions affect other people and relationships.

Preference for Closure as manifested through behavior using S/N or T/F Functions

J=Judging

Want to have an issue or project completed so they can move on; work takes precedence over play; proactive

P=Perceiving

Leave decisions open to modify response in accordance with new information; use play to make work more enjoyable; reactive

---

[107] Compiled from Garst, *Intelligence Types*, 4-9

PART IX
DEFENSIVE MEASURES FOR
INTELLIGENCE

[A]s information becomes more and more a factor of production, of tangible worth for its own sake, the value of the special knowledge that is the essence of intelligence will command a higher price in the global information age marketplace than will the generally available knowledge. Therein lies the most ancient and, at the same time, the most modern challenge to the future of intelligence — protecting it.

— Goodden, in Dearth and Goodden, 415.

Beyond Intelligence Process: Protecting the Means and the Results

An intelligence organization's openness about its validated intelligence methods is of course tempered by self-defense considerations. Two arenas that are complementary to intelligence production, Operations Security (OPSEC) and Information Systems Security (INFOSEC), focus on how practitioners can avoid revealing proprietary or classified information. OPSEC measures protect the specific actions taken to produce intelligence, whereas INFOSEC protects from disclosure the intelligence information used in production, as well as the resulting intelligence products.

In government circles, standard procedures guide the implementation of OPSEC and INFOSEC measures. In the private sector, trial and error may predominate. Companies that emphasize methods for exploiting publicly available information about their competitors may show little regard for protecting themselves from being targeted by the same means they have employed to target others. Furthermore, the trend toward greater computerization of the workplace, including on-line information systems and networked services, makes both government and commercial organizations vulnerable to being exploited themselves.[108]

For example, the Boeing Corporation discovered in 1992 that amateur computer hackers had found their way into the company's computer network, and used stolen passwords to open pathways to proprietary information stored in other computers in industry, government, and education organizations.[109] Prosecuting this case cost Boeing, the FBI, and other law-enforcement authorities considerable time and money.[110] This case was trivial

---

[108] Keen insights into such vulnerabilities are presented in Ira Winkler, *Corporate Espionage: What It Is, Why It Is Happening in Your Company, What You Must Do about It*, (Rocklin, CA: Prima Publishing, 1997).

[109] Rhonda E. MacLean, Senior Manager, Boeing Computing and Communications Security, "The Boeing Hacker Incident," *DODSI Security Awareness Bulletin* Number 1-94 (Richmond, VA: Department of Defense Security Institute, August 1994), 19.

[110] MacLean, 20-21

compared to other well publicized security breaches in government and industry.[111] Yet, at the March 1996 international SCIP conference, of 72 presentations held during four days, only three specifically addressed counterintelligence or security.[112] One reason for this is that businesses may be reluctant to admit their own vulnerabilities in the presence of competitor firms. However, as a Boeing computer security officer has noted, corporations are beginning to realize that admitting flaws in information system defenses is the first step toward preventing future violations, and business and government should work together toward this goal.[113]

In light of the tendency to overlook OPSEC and INFOSEC implementation, the remainder of this section develops an instructional overview of the basic information that government and business personnel should know to protect their activities from unauthorized exploitation. Indeed, for the health of U.S. commerce and national security activities, everyone needs user-friendly information on how to protect proprietary information. Even the most sophisticated corporations have difficulty keeping up with the hazards of the information age; it was not until 1992 that Boeing mandated that all company computer users attend a security awareness briefing, and this was after the firm suffered a major breach of information security. Now Boeing sees "...the importance of information security to our company's long-term competitiveness..." and considers awareness activity as the cornerstone to a good security program.[114]

Operations Security

OPSEC is essential to the intelligence function in both the national security and business environments. OPSEC denies adversaries information about one's own operational capabilities and intentions by identifying, controlling, and protecting indicators associated with the planning and conduct of those operations and other related activities. An adversary is not necessarily a belligerent enemy: In OPSEC terms, an adversary is any entity that acts against one's own interest or actively opposes one's own goals.[115]

To protect an intelligence operation, practitioners can adopt an adversary's perspective. For example, factors at risk in one's own environment can be categorized into critical information, indicators, and vulnerabilities, described briefly below.

---

[111] Examples include those cited in Clifford Stoll, *The Cuckoo's Egg*, (New York: Pocket Books, 1990) and Winn Schwartau, *Information Warfare: Chaos on the Electronic Superhighway*, (New York: Thunder's Mouth Press, 1994).

[112] SCIP, *Conference Proceedings*. Annual International Conference & Exhibit, March 27-30, 1996, (Alexandria, VA: SCIP, March 1996).

[113] MacLean, 22.

[114] MacLean, 22.

[115] National Cryptologic School, Information Security Department, *Operations Security Fundamentals*, (Fort Meade, MD: 1994), 2.

Factors at Risk in Intelligence Operations

Critical Information	Details of capabilities and operations directed against an adversary
Indicator	Detectable actions and publicly available information revealing critical information
Vulnerability	Conditions making exploitable information available to the adversary

Countermeasure options to prevent an adversary from exploiting these factors include: eliminating the indicators altogether, concealing indicator activities, disguising indicator activities, and staging deceptive (false) activities.[116]

The practice of OPSEC is so important to national security that a federal organization has been established as its advocate. As a result of the 1988 Presidential Directive on national operations security, the Interagency OPSEC Support Staff (IOSS) was formed, with the National Security Agency as its director. The core membership of the IOSS includes the Department of Defense, Department of Energy, Central Intelligence Agency, Federal Bureau of Investigation, and General Services Administration.[117] Other executive and national security bodies, including the military services, have representation on the National Operations Security Advisory Committee, which advises the Executive Branch on the practice of OPSEC.[118] The IOSS may be contacted for assistance at:

Interagency OPSEC Support Staff, 6411 Ivy Lane, Suite 400, Greenbelt, MD 20770-1405 Telephone (301) 982-2313/0323.

Information Systems Security

Information Systems Security (INFOSEC) refers to the protection of information that an organization uses and produces in the course of its operations. Today, this means protecting complex electronic networks. Government and business depend upon computerized systems for everything from banking, communications, and data processing to physical security and travel reservations. To the casual observer, INFOSEC may seem the domain of a few technical specialists, or the exclusive concern of the military or intelligence agencies. But INFOSEC is the responsibility of everyone who has ever used a telephone, computer, or automatic bank teller machine.[119]

---

[116] National Cryptologic School, 9.

[117] National Security Agency, Introduction.

[118] National Operations Security Advisory Committee, *National Operations Security Doctrine*, (Greenbelt, MD: Interagency OPSEC Support Staff, January 1993): unnumbered back of first and second physical pages from beginning.

[119] A basic reference on INFOSEC is the National Research Council book *Computers at Risk: Safe Computing in the Information Age*, (Washington, DC: National Academy Press, 1991).

INFOSEC today [involves] significantly more than the traditional security offered by encryption. Network vulnerability to adversarial intercept, tampering, or destruction of data mandates INFOSEC solutions that ensure the authentication, integrity, and availability of classified and unclassified information created, stored, and processed on [information] systems. ... Such solutions must enable the interconnection of Command and Control, intelligence, and support systems and must allow for the commingling of critical information of different classification levels on a common transport backbone. INFOSEC solutions must be flexible, configurable, and result from a risk management scenario that balances the costs and availability of countermeasures against actual threats to, and vulnerabilities of, networks and systems. Finally, INFOSEC must accomplish all of this in an environment in which networks are neither owned nor controlled by [the government] and resources are severely constrained.[120]

Each intelligence organization and activity must tailor its INFOSEC measures to its particular technologies and operational practices, weighing the costs of such measures against their value in safeguarding the mission. A three-dimensional model of INFOSEC, illustrated below, may guide the intelligence service in implementing protective measures and assessing their adequacy. The first dimension addresses the need to understand the vulnerability of information as it passes through different stages of use. The second dimension includes the key characteristics of information that must be preserved for it to remain useful and secure. The third dimension covers the general categories of INFOSEC tools that the intelligence service may employ. Each element of the model is dependent on the others.[121] Together, these interlocking pieces make up a comprehensive INFOSEC strategy appropriate to the public or private sector.

Dimensions of INFOSEC[122]

Information States:	Transmission, Storage, Processing
Critical Information Characteristics:	Confidentiality, Integrity, Availability to Legitimate Users
Countermeasures:	Technology, Policy/Practice, Education

Role of the Federal Government

Federal agencies, including Intelligence Community members, play key roles in helping both government and businesses learn and practice INFOSEC. The two primary authorities for INFOSEC are the Department of Commerce and the Department of

---

[120] National Security Agency, Introduction, para. D.2.
[121] Lynn F. Fisher, "Defining the Threat to Information Systems," *DODSI Security Awareness Bulletin* 2-94, (August 1994), 4.
[122] Fisher.

Defense. Organizations within these departments provide INFOSEC services to their respective constituencies within the framework of national information policies established by the Executive Branch. The following overview begins with a summary of Executive Branch policy.

National Information Policy

The vision of the National Information Infrastructure — or NII — is [as] a vast accessible network of networks that supports communications and information processing to create jobs, increase productivity, improve access to government services, and encourage community networking. The NII is also the wide array of information of all kinds within the networks, whether it is stored, processed, or communicated. Finally, it includes the people... who are today creating and using the NII.[123]

The federal government's role in the NII is to provide a sound legal and policy framework, in conjunction with state, local and Native American governments. Current initiatives include assuring universal service on the NII, thereby enabling open access to government information; protecting intellectual property rights; protecting the privacy of individual information; and stimulating the development of advanced information technologies, including security technologies.[124] The Office of Management and Budget's (OMB) national information security authority covers the development, promotion, implementation and evaluation of government policies and practices for information resource management.[125]

A multi-agency group, the national Information Infrastructure Task Force (IITF), coordinates the federal role in the NII through three committees: the Committee on Applications and Technology, the Telecommunications Policy Committee, and the Information Policy Committee. The OMB's Office of Information and Regulatory Affairs chairs the IITF's Information Policy Committee. As noted below, elements of the Commerce Department chair the other two IITF committees. In addition, the NII Security Issues Forum coordinates NII security activities throughout the IITF and the federal government.[126]

Commerce Department

The Commerce Department's Assistant Secretary for Communications and Information heads the National Telecommunications and Information Administration (NTIA).

---

[123] Sally Katzen, Administrator, Office of Information and Regulatory Affairs, U.S. Office of Management and Budget, Remarks prepared for delivery at the National Computer Security Conference, Baltimore, MD, 11 October 1994.

[124] Katzen.

[125] U.S. Congress, Office of Technology Assessment, *Information Security and Privacy in Network Environments* (Washington, DC: GPO, September 1994), 137.

[126] Katzen

The NTIA's information security responsibilities include: serving as the principal executive adviser to the President on telecommunications and information policy; serving as the principal federal telecommunications research and engineering laboratory, through the Institute for Telecommunication Sciences in Boulder, Colorado; and providing grants to programs that promote the development and provision of advanced telecommunications technologies for the public. The NTIA chairs the IITF's Telecommunications Policy Committee.[127]

The Commerce Department's Technology Administration includes two components involved in information security, the Office of Technology Policy (OTP) and the National Institute for Standards and Technology (NIST).

> The primary role of the OTP is to offer assistance to private sector and government communities in advocating and pursuing policies that maximize the impact of technology on economic growth, and by exercising leadership to define the role of government in supporting U.S. industrial competitiveness in the post-cold war environment. ... NIST's primary mission is to promote U.S. economic growth by working with industry to develop and apply technology, measurements, and standards.[128]

NIST is the national authority for developing government-wide standards and guidelines for protecting unclassified but sensitive information, and for developing government-wide training programs.[129] NIST also chairs the IITF's Committee on Applications and Technology.[130] Finally, NIST maintains the Computer Security Resource Clearinghouse (CSRC) as a resource for anyone with an interest in computer security. It is available on-line 24 hours a day, seven days a week at no charge. The CSRC provides access to crisis response information on security-related threats, vulnerabilities, and solutions, and is a general index to computer security topics such as general risks, privacy, legal issues, viruses, assurance, policy, and training.[131]

Defense Department

The Secretary of Defense is the Executive Agent for National Security Telecommunications and Information Systems Security.[132] As a whole, Department of Defense (DoD) information and communications systems are termed the Defense Information Infrastructure (DII). Under the direction of the Secretary of Defense, three DoD agencies form the

---

[127] Katzen.

[128] Office of the Federal Register, National Archives and Records Administration, *The United States Government Manual 1995/96* (Washington, DC: GPO, 1 July 1995), 167-168.

[129] U.S. Congress, Office of Technology Assessment, 13.

[130] Katzen.

[131] Defense Information Systems Agency (DISA), "The NIST Computer Security Resource Clearinghouse," *DISSPatch* 4, no. 1 (3rd Quarter 1996): 6. See CSRC home page at: http://www.csrc.nist.gov.

[132] National Security Agency, Chapter 3, B.d.

core DII INFOSEC team: the Defense Intelligence Agency (DIA), the Defense Information Systems Agency (DISA), and the National Security Agency (NSA). Although notionally the DII is a dedicated system for proprietary and classified national defense information, in fact over 95 percent of its communications are carried on the public switched networks of the NII.[133] Thus, DoD expertise in information security doctrine and technology makes the organizations explained below key resources for other government organizations and for the private sector.

The Defense Intelligence Agency, as the central authority for military intelligence, provides INFOSEC threat analysis and support to the DII.[134] Another agency, DISA, is responsible for planning, developing, and supporting command, control, communications, and information systems that serve the needs of the National Command Authorities under all conditions of peace and war; it further ensures the interoperability of all DII systems and those national and/or international commercial systems that affect the DISA mission.[135] NSA acts as the National Manager for National Security Telecommunications and Information Systems Security in the name of the Secretary of Defense. In this capacity, NSA is the focal point for U.S. government cryptography and for the security of national security telecommunications and information systems.[136] NSA provides DISA with the tools, techniques, products, services, and security management structures to protect the DII, through its "V" Group, the customer service and engineering organization for information systems security.[137] Within NSA, the National Computer Security Center (NCSC) conducts technical evaluation of the protection capabilities of commercially produced and supported systems.[138] Through its Information Systems Security Research Joint Technology Office (ISSR-JTO), NSA coordinates with DISA and the DoD's Advanced Research Projects Agency on engineering INFOSEC technologies. The ISSR-JTO provides a first line of defense for defensive information warfare, and permits electronic commerce between DoD and its contractors. It also maintains research and technology interfaces with the military departments, national labs, universities, and industry.[139] NSA coordinates with the National Institute for Standards and Technology (NIST) in matters of common concern.[140] Together, DIA, DISA, and NSA operate the DoD Center for Information Systems Security.[141]

---

[133] LtGen Kenneth A. Minihan, "Intelligence and Information System Security," *Defense Intelligence Journal* 5, no. 1 (Spring 1996): 20.

[134] Defense Information Systems Agency, "INFOSEC and the DII," *DISSPatch* 4, No. 1, (3rd Quarter, CY 1996): 7.

[135] Office of the Federal Register, 234.

[136] NSA, Chapter 3, B.e.(2).

[137] DISA, "Introducing NSA's New and Improved V Group," *DISSPatch* 4, no. 3 (3rd Quarter 1996): 2.

[138] NSA, Chapter 6, para. 1.

[139] DISA, "V Group," 5.

[140] INFOSEC Program Management Office (IPMO), *DISSPatch*, May 97, 14.

[141] DISA, "INFOSEC and the DII," *DISSPatch* 4, No. 1 (3rd Quarter 1996): 7.

The Department of Defense's INFOSEC Program Management Office (IPMO) is a joint DoD/DISA/NSA organization charged with executing centrally managed INFOSEC functions within the DoD.[142] The IPMO provides operational protection and detection capability for the DII against information exploitation, manipulation, or destruction. It administers DoD-wide INFOSEC training and manages the DoD INFOSEC Technical Services Contract. The IPMO conducts vulnerability, threat, and operational analyses of the DII, provides security policy guidance and oversight to DISA programs, and certifies DISA and non-DISA systems that connect to the DII.[143] The IPMO also provides support to the Assistant Secretary of Defense for Command, Control, Communications, Computers, Intelligence, Surveillance and Reconnaissance (ASD/C4ISR).[144] Another DoD body, chaired by the ASD/C4ISR, also has a role in INFOSEC. Under the purview of the National Security Council, the National Security Telecommunications and Information Systems Security Committee (NSTISSC) advises Executive Branch agencies and Departments on the status of national security systems. Its two subcommittees focus on telecommunications security and information systems security, respectively. NSA provides the NSTISSC secretariat.[145]

In addition, the DoD Security Institute (DODSI) promotes security awareness and compliance with security procedures in DoD by offering training courses to security personnel in DoD and DoD-related industry, publishing security awareness bulletins, and disseminating information to security trainers on security and counterintelligence.[146]

INFOSEC for Everyone

The national authorities for INFOSEC described above evolved out of the need to protect the fundamental role of information in a democratic society and market economy. They help strike the balance between free exchange of information and privacy, and between free enterprise and regulation. Government-sponsored information policy and technology set the standards upon which nearly every facet of public and private life is based. Citizens receive basic services through government-created or -regulated information infrastructure, including automatic payroll deposit to employee bank accounts, cellular telephone service, electronic commerce via the Internet, air and rail traffic control, emergency medical services, and electrical power supply.

Such services contribute not only to the citizen's quality of life, but to the very functioning of the nation. Information is the lifeblood of society and the economy. Imagine the chaos that would reign if the government, the military, banks, businesses, schools, and hospitals could not communicate reliably. Life would come to a halt.

---

[142] IPMO, 14.

[143] DISA, "INFOSEC," 7.

[144] U.S. Department of Defense Security Institute (DODSI), *DODSI Security Awareness Bulletin* 2-94 (August 1994): 25.

[145] NSA, Chapter 3, B.a, B.b, and B.c.

[146] DODSI, front cover, 12, 18.

INFOSEC is designed to protect society from inadvertent or intentional harm to these key functions. The same free access to information that makes society flourish also makes it vulnerable to damage, attack or exploitation. For example, passive threats such as shoddy equipment, faulty software, or negligent personnel can disrupt service and destroy information. Hostile threats include thrill-seeking computer hackers and belligerent foreign adversaries who deliberately target sensitive government and public information networks with the aim of disrupting or destroying key operations, such as military projects or power grids.[147] Comparable scenarios within the business sector, to include information sabotage and deception actions against competitors, are at least plausible. Therefore, basic knowledge of INFOSEC may benefit citizens in all walks of life. Addresses and phone numbers for the INFOSEC agencies that can assist the public are listed at the end of this chapter.[148]

Government expertise in information technology and policy has made it the authority specifically on protecting intelligence operations. The private sector may also benefit from this expertise by applying INFOSEC measures in business intelligence. In brief, successful intelligence operations rely on secure transmission, storage, and processing of the information used. The information itself must be exchanged only among legitimate users, and it must retain its intended meaning and be available to users upon demand. Finally, intelligence information and products can be protected through technology (access control, encryption), through security policies and practices, and through educating the workforce, as with this document.

Points of contact:

Commerce Department:
NIST, Public Inquiries Unit, 100 Bureau Drive, Gaithersburg, MD 20899-0001; 301-975-6478 (voice); email: inquiries@*nist.gov*; Website: *http://www.nist.gov/*.

DoD:
IPMO, 5111 Leesburg Pike, Suite 100, Falls Church, VA 22014-3206; 703-681-7944/DSN761-7944 (voice); 703-681-1386/DSN 703-761-1386 (fax); e-mail: *cissa@ncr.disa.mil*, Website: *http://www.disa.mil/ciss*.

DISA, Public Affairs Office, 701 South Courthouse Road, Arlington, VA 22204-2199; 703-607-6900 (voice); Website: *http://www.disa.mil*.

DODSI, 8000 Jefferson Davis Highway, Building 33E, Richmond, VA 23297-5091; 804-279-5314/DSN 695-5314 (voice); 804-279-5239/DSN 695-5239 (fax).

---

[147] Gregory L. Vistica and Evan Thomas, "The Secret Hacker Wars, Behind the spreading battle over cyberterrorism," *Newsweek* (1 June 1998): 60.

[148] In addition, the National Counterintelligence Center provides support to the private sector regarding economic espionage, economic intelligence collection, and threat awareness. The NACIC website is *http://www.nacis.gov*.

NCSC, Suite 6765, 9800 Savage Road, Fort George G. Meade, MD 20755-6765; 20 410-859-4371 (voice); 410-859-4375 (fax).

NSA, Fort George G. Meade, MD 20755-6000, Attn: V1, Office of Customer Support Services; 410-859-4384/DSN 644-0111; 800-688-6115 (voice); Website: *http:// www.nsa.gov:8080/.*

EPILOGUE

This primer has reviewed government intelligence production practices in building-block fashion. It has also explored the defensive measures comprising information security and operations security, which are integral to all the building blocks, and are equally applicable to private businesses and government organizations. Finally, the primer has drawn a cognitive, behavioral and personality profile of the central figure in intelligence production — the intelligence analyst. In the spirit of benchmarking, this document invites a reciprocal examination of best practices that may have been developed by private businesses, and of principles that may have been derived from other academic studies of intelligence-related processes.

Although this effort reflects a government initiative, in fact the government Intelligence Community may receive the greater share of rewards from benchmarking its own process. Potential benefits to the Community include an improved public image, increased self-awareness, more efficient recruitment through more informed self-selection by candidates for employment, as well as any resultant acquisition of specialized information from subject matter experts in the business and academic communities.

Primary advantages for the government's partners in the exchange of information on best practices could be greater understanding of how tax dollars are spent, and the opportunity to transfer an appreciation of government professional intelligence production, security, and staffing methods into academic curricula and business operations.

For all participants in benchmarking, releasing information is actually a way of controlling it, a way of depicting and fostering an accurate organizational image rather than allowing others to draw and disseminate erroneous characterizations. For the U.S. Intelligence Community in particular, any initiative in benchmarking the intelligence process fulfills a charge of the recently completed Report on the Community's Roles and Capabilities: to improve its performance through closer relationships with customers, including the private sector.

GLOSSARY

ASD/C4ISR	Assistant Secretary of Defense for Command, Control, Communications, Computers, Intelligence, Surveillance and Reconnaissance
BI	Business Intelligence
CIA	Central Intelligence Agency
CISS	Center for Information Systems Security
CSRC	Computer Security Resource Center
DCI	Director of Central Intelligence
DIA	Defense Intelligence Agency
DII	Defense Information Infrastructure
DISA	Defense Information Systems Agency
DoD	Department of Defense
DODSI	Department of Defense Security Institute
FISINT	Foreign Instrumentation and Signature Intelligence
GPO	U.S. Government Printing Office
HUMINT	Human Intelligence
IC	Intelligence Community
IITF	Information Infrastructure Task Force
IMINT	Imagery Intelligence
INFOSEC	Information Systems Security
INFOWAR	Information Warfare
IOSS	Interagency OPSEC Support Staff
IPMO	INFOSEC Program Management Office
ISSR-JTO	Information Systems Security Research Joint Technology Office
JIVA	Joint Intelligence Virtual Architecture

JMIC	Joint Military Intelligence College
MASINT	Measurement and Signature Intelligence
MBTI	Myers-Briggs Type Indicator
MRI	Management Research Institute
NACIC	National Counterintelligence Center
NCSC	National Computer Security Center
NIC	National Intelligence Council
NII	National Information Infrastructure
NIMA	National Imagery and Mapping Agency
NIST	National Institute for Standards and Technology
NSA	National Security Agency
NSTISSC	National Security Telecommunications and Information Systems Security Committee
NTIA	National Telecommunications and Information Administration
OMB	Office of Management and Budget
OPSEC	Operations Security
OSD	Office of the Secretary of Defense
OTP	Office of Technology Policy
SCIP	Society of Competitive Intelligence Professionals
SIGINT	Signals Intelligence

BIBLIOGRAPHY

Allen, George. "The Professionalization of Intelligence." In *Strategic Intelligence: Theory and Application*, 2d ed. Eds. Douglas H. Dearth and R. Thomas Goodden, 33-40. Washington, DC: Joint Military Intelligence Training Center (JMITC), 1995.

Andre, Louis E. "Intelligence Production: Towards a Knowledge-Based Future." *Defense Intelligence Journal* 6, no. 2 (Fall 1997): 35-45.

Babbie, Earl. *The Practice of Social Research.* Belmont, CA: Wadsworth Publishing Co, 1992.

Ben-Israel, Isaac. "Philosophy and Methodology of Intelligence: The Logic of Estimative Process." *Intelligence and National Security* 4, no. 4 (October 1989): 660-718.

Brei, Captain William S. *Getting Intelligence Right: The Power of Logical Procedure.* Occasional Paper Number Two. Washington, DC: Joint Military Intelligence College (JMIC), January 1996.

Carney, LT Donald J., USN. *Estimating the Dissolution of Yugoslavia.* Seminar Paper. Washington, DC: Joint Military Intelligence College, September 1991.

Central Intelligence Agency. *A Compendium of Analytic Tradecraft Notes.* Washington, DC, Directorate of Intelligence, February 1997.

_____. *A Consumer's Guide to Intelligence.* Washington, DC: Public Affairs Staff, July 1995. PAS 95-00010.

Clauser, Jerome K. and Sandra M. Weir. *Intelligence Research Methodology, An Introduction to Techniques and Procedures for Conducting Research in Defense Intelligence.* Washington, DC: Defense Intelligence School, 1975.

D'Aveni, Richard. "Hypercompetition." Briefing to SCIP Conference. Alexandria, VA, 28 March 1996.

Davis, Jack. "Combatting Mindset." *Studies in Intelligence* 35, no. 4 (Winter 1991): 13-18.

_____. *Intelligence Changes in Analytic Tradecraft in CIA's Directorate of Intelligence.* Washington, DC: CIA Directorate of Intelligence, April 1995.

_____. *The Challenge of Opportunity Analysis.* Intelligence Monograph. Washington, DC: Center for the Study of Intelligence, July 1992. CSI 92-003U.

Davis-Floyd, Robbie E. "Storytelling Corporate Futures: The Shell Scenarios." *International Journal of Futures Studies* 1 (1995-1997), on-line at http://www.systems.org/HTML/journals.htm, accessed 3 December 1997.

Dearth, Douglas H. "National Intelligence: Profession and Process." In *Strategic Intelligence: Theory and Application*, 2d ed. Eds. Douglas H. Dearth and R. Thomas Goodden, 15-31. Washington, DC: JMITC, 1995.

_____. "The Politics of Intelligence." In *Strategic Intelligence: Theory and Application*, 2d ed. Eds. Douglas H. Dearth and R. Thomas Goodden, 97-121. Washington, DC: JMITC, 1995.

Defense Information Systems Agency. "INFOSEC and the DII." *DISSPatch* 4, no. 1 (3rd Quarter 1996): 7.

_____. "Introducing NSA's New and Improved V Group." *DISSPatch* 4, no. 1 (3rd Quarter 1996): 2, 5.

_____. "The NIST Computer Security Resource Clearinghouse." *DISSPatch* 4, no. 1 (3rd Quarter 1996): 6.

Defense Intelligence Agency. *Vector 21, A Strategic Plan for the Defense Intelligence Agency*. Washington, DC: Programs and Operations Staff, undated.

Elmuti, Dean, and Hanus Kathawaia and Scott J. Lloyed. "The Benchmarking Process: Assessing Its Value and Limitations." *Industrial Management*, 39, No. 4 (July/August 1997): 12-19.

Fisher, Lynn F. "Defining the Threat to Information Systems." *DODSI Security Awareness Bulletin* 2-94 (August 1994): 3-10.

Frankenfield, Jerry and Melissie Rumizen. *A Guide to Benchmarking*. Fort Meade, MD: NSA, 12 July 1995.

Garst, Ronald D. "Components of Intelligence." In *A Handbook of Intelligence Analysis*, 2d ed. Ed. Ronald D. Garst, 1-32. Washington, DC: Defense Intelligence College, January 1989.

_____. *Intelligence Types: The Role of Personality in the Intelligence Profession*. Washington, DC: Joint Military Intelligence College, August 1995.

Goodden, Royal Thomas. "Intelligence in the Information Age." In *Strategic Intelligence: Theory and Application*, 2d ed. Eds. Douglas H. Dearth and R. Thomas Goodden, 409-416. Washington, DC: JMITC, 1995.

Harkleroad, David. "Actionable CI." Briefing to SCIP Conference. Alexandria, VA, 28 March 1996.

Harris, Gary. "Evaluating Intelligence Evidence." In *A Handbook of Intelligence Analysis*, 2d ed. Ed. Ronald D. Garst, 33-48. Washington, DC: Defense Intelligence College, January 1989.

Haucke, Mark H. Industrial Psychologist, National Security Agency. Interview with the author, 25 May 1995.

Hecht, Francoise. "The Aha! Factor." *Director* 50, No. 12 (July 1997): 59.

Herring, Jan. "Strides in Institutionalizing BI in Businesses." Briefing to SCIP Conference. Alexandria, VA, 28 March 1996.

Hulnick, Arthur S. "The Intelligence Producer-Policy Consumer Linkage: A Theoretical Approach." *Intelligence and National Security*, 1, No. 2, (May 1986): 212-233.

_____. "Managing Intelligence Analysis: Strategies for Playing the End Game." *International Journal of Intelligence and CounterIntelligence*, 2, No. 3, (Fall 1988): 321-343.

Hunter, Douglas E. *Political/Military Applications of Bayesian Analysis: Methodological Issues.* Boulder, CO: Westview, 1984.

Johnson, Loch K. *America's Secret Power, The CIA in a Democratic Society.* New York: Oxford University Press, 1989.

Jones, Morgan D. *The Thinker's Toolkit.* New York: Random House, 1995: 44-46.

Kahaner, Larry. *Competitive Intelligence: From Black Ops to Boardrooms.* New York: Simon and Schuster, 1996.

Kam, Ephraim. *Surprise Attack.* Cambridge, MA: Harvard University Press, 1988.

Kaplan, Abraham. *The Conduct of Inquiry.* San Francisco, CA: Chandler, 1964.

Katzen, Sally. Administrator, Office of Information and Regulatory Affairs, U.S. Office of Management and Budget. Remarks prepared for delivery at the National Computer Security Conference, Baltimore, Maryland, 11 October 1994.

Keesing, Hugo A. Instructor, Joint Military Intelligence College. Remarks to a meeting of the Communications Analysis Association, Fort Meade, MD, 6 November 1995.

Keirsey, David. *Portraits of Temperament.* Amherst, NY: Prometheus, 1987.

Kight, Leila. "Elements of CI Success." Briefing to SCIP Conference. Alexandria, VA, 28 March, 1996.

Macdaid, Gerald P., Mary H. McCaulley and Richard I. Kainz. *Myers-Briggs Type Indicator: Atlas of Type Tables.* Gainesville, FL: Center for Applications of Psychological Type, 1986.

MacLean, Rhonda E. "The Boeing Hacker Incident." *DODSI Security Awareness Bulletin* 2-94 (August 1994): 19-22.

Major, James S. *Briefing with Intelligence.* Washington DC: Joint Military Intelligence College, August 1997.

_____. *The Style Guide: Research and Writing at the Joint Military Intelligence College*. Washington DC: Joint Military Intelligence College, August 1994.

Management Research Institute (MRI). *Ability and Knowledge Requirements*. Bethesda, MD: MRI, 1994.

_____. *Job Dimension Ratings*. Performance evaluation booklet. Bethesda, MD: Management Research Institute, 1995.

Mathams, R. H. "The Intelligence Analyst's Notebook." In *Strategic Intelligence: Theory and Application*, 2d ed. Eds. Douglas H. Dearth and R. Thomas Goodden, 77-96. Washington, DC: JMITC, 1995.

Minihan, Lt. Gen. Kenneth A. Director, National Security Agency. "DIR Addresses the Future of NSA." *Communicator* 4, no. 20 (14 May 1996): 1-3.

_____. "Intelligence and Information System Security." *Defense Intelligence Journal* 5, no. 1 (Spring 1996): 13-23.

_____. "Winning the Information Game: NSA's Role in the 21st Century." *NSA Newsletter*, May 1996, 3.

Moyer, Kathy. "Scenario Planning at British Airways — A Case Study." *Long Range Planning* 29, No. 2 (April 1996): 172-181.

Murray, Thomas H. "Taxonomy of Problem Types." Analytic coursework material for the Joint Military Intelligence College, based upon Morgan D. Jones, *The Thinker's Toolkit*. New York: Random House, 1995: 44-46.

Myers, Isabel Briggs. *Introduction to Type*. Palo Alto, CA: Consulting Psychologists Press, 1980.

_____. and Mary H. McCaulley. *Manual: A Guide to the Development and Use of the Myers-Briggs Type Indicator*. Palo Alto, CA: Consulting Psychologists Press, 1985.

_____. with Peter Myers. *Gifts Differing*. Palo Alto, CA: Consulting Psychologists Press, 1980.

National Cryptologic School (NCS). Information Security Department, *Operations Security Fundamentals*. Fort Meade, MD: NCS, 1993.

National Operations Security (OPSEC) Advisory Committee. *National Operations Security Doctrine*. Greenbelt, MD: Interagency OPSEC Support Staff, January 1993.

National Research Council. *Computers at Risk: Safe Computing in the Information Age*. Washington, DC: National Academy Press, 1991.

National Security Agency. *1995 INFOSEC Manual*. Fort Meade, MD: NSA, 1995.

Office of the Federal Register. National Archives and Records Administration. *The United States Government Manual 1995/96*. Washington, DC: GPO, 1 July 1995.

P.L. 102-183. "David L. Boren National Security Education Act of 1991." Title VIII, Sections 801-802, 4 December 1991.

P.L. 103-62. "Government Performance and Results Act of 1993."

Peterson, Marilyn. *Applications in Criminal Analysis*. Westport, Connecticut: Greenwood Press, 1994.

Prescott, John. Professor of Business Administration, University of Pittsburgh. "Research." Briefing to SCIP Conference, 28 March 1996

Rumizen, Melissie C. Benchmarking Manager, National Security Agency. Interviews with the author, 4 January 1996 and 5 July 1996.

Schmidlin, LCDR William G., USN. *Zen and the Art of Intelligence Analysis*. MSSI Thesis. Washington, DC: Joint Military Intelligence College, July 1993.

Schum, David A. *Evidence and Inference for the Intelligence Analyst*. Volume I. Lanham, MD: University Press of America, 1987.

Schwartau, Winn. *Information Warfare: Chaos on the Electronic Superhighway*. New York: Thunder's Mouth Press, 1994.

SCIP. *1995 SCIP Membership Directory*. Alexandria, VA: SCIP, 1995.

_____. *Competitive Intelligence Review* 8, No. 3 (Fall 1997): unnumbered 8th page.

_____. *Conference Proceedings*. Annual International Conference & Exhibit, March 27-30, 1996. Alexandria, VA: SCIP, March 1996.

Smith, Ian. "Avoiding Future Shock." *Director* 50, No. 12 (July 1997): 56-59.

Stoll, Clifford. *The Cuckoo's Egg*. New York: Pocket Books, 1990.

Studeman, William O. "Leading Intelligence Along the Byways of Our Future: Acquiring C⁴ISR Architectures for the 21st Century." *Defense Intelligence Journal* 7, no. 1 (Spring 1998): 47-65.

Swenson, Russell G. *An Office Manager's Guide to Intelligence Readiness*. Occasional Paper Number Three. Washington, DC: JMIC, December 1996.

Tetzlaff, Jonathan. Area Director, Security Research and Analysis, Amoco Corporation. Personal correspondence with editor, 24 October 1997.

Turner, Michael A. "Setting Analytical Priorities in U.S. Intelligence." *International Journal of Intelligence and CounterIntelligence* 9, no. 3 (Fall 1996): 313-327.

U.S. Congress, House Permanent Select Committee on Intelligence. *IC21: The Intelligence Community in the 21st Century.* Staff Study, April 1996: Section III, "Intelligence Requirements Process."

_____. Office of Technology Assessment. *Information Security and Privacy in Network Environments.* Washington, DC: GPO, September 1994. OTA-TCT-60

_____. *Preparing for the 21st Century: An Appraisal of U.S. Intelligence.* Report of the Commission on the Roles and Capabilities of the U.S. Intelligence Community. Washington, DC: GPO, 1 March 1996.

U.S. Department of Defense. DoD Security Institute (DODSI). *DODSI Security Awareness Bulletin* 2-94 (August 1994).

_____. Joint Chiefs of Staff. Joint Pub 1-02. *Dictionary of Military and Associated Terms.* Washington, DC: 23 March 1994: 184.

_____. Joint Chiefs of Staff. Joint Pub 2-0. *Joint Doctrine for Intelligence Support to Operations.* Washington, DC: GPO, 5 May 1995.

Vistica, Gregory L. and Evan Thomas, "The Secret Hacker Wars, Behind the Spreading Battle Over Cyberterrorism." *Newsweek* (1 June 1998): 60.

Westerfield, H. Bradford. "Inside Ivory Bunkers: CIA Analysts Resist Managers" Pandering' — Part I." *International Journal of Intelligence and CounterIntelligence* 9, no. 4 (Winter 1996/97): 407-424.

_____. "Inside Ivory Bunkers: CIA Analysts Resist Managers' "Pandering' — Part II." *International Journal of Intelligence and CounterIntelligence* 10, no. 1 (Spring 1997): 19-54.

White House. *National Operations Security Program.* Fact Sheet. Washington, DC: January 1988.

Winkler, Ira. *Corporate Espionage: What It Is, Why It Is Happening in Your Company, What You Must Do about It.* Rocklin, CA: Prima Publishing, 1997.

ABOUT THE AUTHOR

Lisa Krizan has been a researcher with the Department of Defense since 1987. She received a master's degree from the Joint Military Intelligence College in 1996 and developed many of the ideas for this paper as part of her thesis on benchmaking the intelligence process. A second-generation intelligence scholar, she follows the example set by her father, 1972 Defense Intelligence College graduate Allen J. Montecino, Jr., Colonel, USAF (Ret).

Joint Military Intelligence College
Occasional Papers

1. Classified paper.

2. *Getting Intelligence Right: The Power of Logical Procedure*, Capt (USAF) William S. Brei, 1996.

3. *An Office Manager's Guide to Intelligence Readiness*, Russell G. Swenson, 1996.

4. Classified paper.

5. *A Flourishing Craft: Teaching Intelligence Studies,* Papers Prepared for the 18 June 1999 JMIC Conference on Teaching Intelligence Studies at Colleges and Universities, 1999.

6. *Intelligence Essentials for Everyone*, Lisa Krizan, 1999.